Grappling with Your Identity

Clinging to the Rock

Lynne Fox

TO MY HUSBAND

What a delight!

I look in your eyes and see the heart of my Lord.

Table of Contents

Appreciation
Foreword
Why This Book
Delight

Part I - Falling Short and Faking It
Overview
Chapter 1 - Self-Confusion / 5
Chapter 2 - Somebody Besides Me / 9
Chapter 3 - Identity Problems / 13

Part II - Real Worth and Pseudoworth
Overview
Chapter 4 - Spirit, Wind, and Breath: Identity and God / 25
Chapter 5 - Blowing into Mud Pies: Identity and Adam / 31
Chapter 6 - Our Invisible Self: Identity and Us / 37
Chapter 7 - Differentiating Self from Stuff / 47
Chapter 8 - Differentiating Self from Activity / 55
Chapter 9 - Differentiating Self from Others / 59

Part III - Death Begins
Overview
Chapter 10 - The Entrance of Death / 71
Chapter 11 - The Spread of Death / 77

Part IV - Life Begins Again: A New Identity
Overview
Chapter 12 - Spiritual Beings, Made in God's Image / 85
Chapter 13 - Made Alive by God's Breath / 93
Chapter 14 - New Creations, in Earthen Houses / 101
Chapter 15 - Complete / 105
Chapter 16 - And Doubtful / 109

Part V - Blindness to Sight

Overview

Chapter 17 - Blind Men Walking / 117

Chapter 18 - Pirates, Mirrors, and Glory / 121

Chapter 19 - Expectations and Exhaustion / 131

Chapter 20 - Double Vision, Single Self / 141

Chapter 21 - Not Self but Sin / 149

Chapter 22 - Double World, Single Focus / 161

Part VI - Authenticity and Dignity

Overview

Chapter 23 - Being Who We Are / 169

Chapter 24 - Being Me at the Airport / 179

APPRECIATION

Although I've written the text of this book, I really can't claim credit for the ideas behind it. Ted Wise, a good shepherd, taught me the basics of the identity shift that takes place when a person accepts God's gift of life through Jesus Christ. He answered my questions, taught me to depend on the truth of Scripture, and challenged me to apply that truth to the nitty-gritty of my life. Without your teaching, Ted, this book could never have come into being. Without your discipling, I would still be ashamed of who I am. You know my gratitude.

And to the many who have listened, challenged, and encouraged me as I've worked to put years of pastoring onto the printed page – you have generously given me time, support, discerning guidance, and, above all, friendship. My appreciation exceeds words.

To God be the glory. I do love You! May my words reflect Your Word.

Author Lynne Fox, Psy.D, has served as Counseling Pastor at Peninsula Bible Church, Palo Alto, CA since 1992. Her ability to apply scripture to the details of life enriches her counseling and teaching ministry as well as her training of lay-counselors and pastors.

FOREWORD

The subject of our identity in Christ has been sadly neglected and misunderstood; the need for biblical teaching on identity continues to be urgent. It was, then, with pleasure that I read Lynne Fox's development of this important part of our lives as Jesus' disciples.

Her book, *Grappling with Your Identity*, flows smoothly forward as Lynne builds stone-upon-stone to structure her case for a biblically based perspective on the new self that God creates. Her personal transparency is engaging, as is her writing style. She has offered us something of value. She has written well.

Elaine Stedman

Why This Book

"My only regret in life is that I'm not someone else." So said Woody Allen. Has his regret ever crossed your mind? Problems with self-worth are rampant and potentially devastating, sometimes masked, but rarely absent. Woody Allen was right: every person needs a new self. *Grappling with Your Identity* reveals how that miracle happens.

Our ravenous hunger for self-esteem has generated numerous books on self-worth, books that promise much but don't deliver the goods. Their recommendations about self-effort and behavioral change can't solve our inner fear of falling short and being shamed. Most of us, including most Christians, identify with every ugly thing we do. We think our flaws define us. There's a better option.

Knowing who we are because of Christ is crucial. Christians may have become new inside, but most don't believe it. And, until we believe it, our old behaviors will never change. We can't live a new life if we think we're still an old self. By convincing us that we, at salvation, have partaken of God's magnificence, *Grappling with Your Identity* gives us the foundation to lead a new life by explaining our new identity in Christ.

In this biblically based book, you'll find out *who* defines us – not people but God – and *what* defines us – not a changed lifestyle but a changed self. You'll learn *how* we change when we receive Christ, *why* we doubt this change, and *how* to turn from doubt and shame to delight in our new identity in the Lord. As you read, you'll know you're acceptable; when you finish, you'll feel clean.

DELIGHT

If you've ever seen a wedding, you know the scenario: the bride appears, the first notes of the Bridal Chorus ring out, and every head turns in unison to watch her walk down the aisle towards her groom. Every head except mine. I watch the groom.

I study the delight on his face, the intensity of his love, his penetrating gaze that drinks in her presence, the way every fiber of his being is aware only of her. I long to be looked at this way – and so do you.

Few Christians believe that the Lord savors us with such delight. But He does. Look:

> *It will no longer be said to you, "Forsaken," ...but you will be called, "My delight is in her," ...for the LORD delights in you... and as the bridegroom rejoices over the bride, your God will rejoice over you (Isaiah 62:4-5)*

> *Shout for joy, O daughter of Zion! Shout in triumph, O Israel! Rejoice and exult with all your heart, O daughter of Jerusalem! The LORD has taken away His judgments against you, He has cleared away your enemies. The King of Israel, the LORD, is in your midst; you will fear disaster no more. In that day it will be said to Jerusalem: "Do not be afraid, O Zion; do not let your hands fall limp." The LORD your God is in your midst, a victorious warrior. He will exult over you with joy, He will be quiet in His love, He will rejoice over you with shouts of joy. (Zephaniah 3:14-17)*

It's right there in black and white: the Lord delights in you; He rejoices over you as a bridegroom rejoices over his bride.

As you read this book, I pray that you will walk towards the Lord, look full in His face, and savor His delight.

PART I
Falling Short
and
Faking It

Part I Overview
Falling Short and Faking It

Occasionally, after a stunning success, we bask in others' approval. Yet far too often we fall short of our goal and fail to receive the affirmation for which we hunger. At those times, the uneasy times, people and circumstances, not to mention our own self-judgmental thoughts, generate a nagging fear that we are flawed to the core. Most of us doubt our self-worth.

Such self-doubt spawns a host of unwise choices. We begin with self-absorption (which only increases our awareness of our failures), move into a quest to improve ourselves (good luck), and end up with various phony roles behind which we hide. We turn falling short into faking it. We're wasting our time: self-effort won't rid us of self-doubt.

The first part of this book details our predicament. Chapter 1, *Self-Confusion*, exposes our doubt of our worth and our confusion about who we are. Chapter 2, *Somebody Besides Me*, shows us the need to be aware of others. Chapter 3, *Identity Problems*, unmasks the roles behind which we hide and assures us that God gives us worth that won't disappear, even when we fail.

What if, when we fall short, we no longer have to fake it?

1
Self-Confusion

Most of us are pretty confused about who we are. Some of us applaud ourselves, and some of us put ourselves down, but most of us shift back and forth between the two, not quite able to hold on to either position. Consistency is not one of our strengths.

Other people don't help much; they aren't that consistent either. Nobody around us, however loyal or well-intentioned, ever goes more than a few days (maybe a few weeks) before failing, sometimes remarkably, to give us the approval we so desire. A sharp comment, a frown, a questionable laugh, an unexpected silence – each unpredictably punctures our self-confidence, and suddenly we wonder if we really are a loser, and if everyone else has known it for years. Our self-perception tends to shift with the company we keep.

This inconsistent affirmation from others might be manageable if we could only hike up our own socks and stride forward with confident dignity. But we can't. Sure, we can get short bursts of self-admiration, but nothing reliable. Rarely do any of us go for long without screwing something up, all too often glaringly and publicly. And then we wonder again if we really are a loser, and wonder if others have noticed.

All this leaves us uncertain of our worth, suspicious that we fall short of the ideal (whatever that is), and convinced that we need to work harder to produce a better product.

I have a lot of experience in this area. I spent years trying to produce an appealing identity. Mine became a sort of self-affirming quest that moved me into an unusual form of idolatry – I made an idol out of Walter Mitty.

WALTER'S STORY

You may not have heard of Walter. Walter was the champion of James Thurber's 1939 short story, *The Secret Life of Walter Mitty*. A mousy little character, Walter lived in a suffocatingly bland real world but managed to escape that world by ignoring it. Instead, he created his own reality, a virtual reality, and there he played the hero. Inside his head, Walter acted in a series of stunning self-directed fantasies all featuring his amazing accomplishments. He may have been nothing to the people around him, but to himself, Walter was a star.

Aside from his problem of indulging in obviously delusional behavior, Walter had a point: his fantasies about himself were clearly more appealing than his real personality. I *get* that. So do you. We all try to picture ourselves as more fascinating than we suspect we really are.

And that's where my idolatry of Walter Mitty came in.

I found Walter a compelling role model, because I fantasized too. I fantasized a lot, and for a very good reason: it was so reassuring. In my fantasies, I ran my own mental movies where I displayed my wit, cleverness, and skill and routinely found my audience breaking into wild applause. My fantasies were great events.

Real life wasn't as much fun. In real life, I kept noticing my failures, and when I wasn't noticing them, I worried about them. Walter Mitty never screwed up and he never worried, at least not in his imagination. But me? I noticed my failures and I worried about them – I couldn't even live up to my idol.

Come to think of it, though, Walter wasn't that good a role model. His real life was probably no better than mine. He may have imagined fantastic exploits, but I'll bet a sharp comment from Mrs. Mitty could instantly interrupt his daydreams and grind his carefully crafted self-esteem into the dirt. I'll bet that his sense of self was as confused as mine. Or perhaps yours.

Mrs. Mitty's put-downs obviously didn't help Walter's quest for a dependable sense of self-worth, but neither did his own upbeat imagination. We can relate. Human input, our own or others', hasn't done much for our self-esteem either.

WHAT WALTER OVERLOOKED

Walter had an identity problem, and so do we. But what if you and I had something Walter was missing? What if we didn't have to rely on delusions to feel worthwhile? What if we had something trustworthy, outside of our imaginations, which assured us of our value, something to cling to when people or circumstances or our own perceptions plunged us into confusion and insecurity?

The Bible is that something. I love this book. I love its consistency. To discover something so practical, so powerful, so dependable, so beyond human, and so, well, consistent is very appealing. I can hang on to its words; I can count on them to give me a grip on reality. God's words protect me from stumbling over all that inconsistent human input and ending up confused about who I am.

But I don't love the Bible just because its pages say wonderful things. I love it because Somebody is behind those pages. Somebody besides me. I'm not alone when I read. Somebody is there loving me and communicating to me. God is speaking, and the conversation turns out to be intensely personal.

For starters, He tells me about my incredible worth. And, to protect me from getting stuck on myself, He tells me that everyone else has the same value I do. I'm to remember that. I'm to notice their worth and delight in it. The point is not to get stuck on myself, but to get over myself, to notice others and to love them.

Being sure of our worth allows us to love people and to love God. It's an essential. For until we know we're worthwhile, we'll never stop guarding and grooming ourselves, never be free of our self-centered fantasies, and never start caring for others.

Knowing our worth gives us the confidence to pay attention to others. It lets us value "somebody besides me."

2
Somebody
Besides Me

Knowing who I am settles an issue that's taken up a great deal of my energy: self-absorption.

If I know I'm okay – I mean if I'm absolutely certain of it – then the issue of my identity no longer requires my attention. Knowing my value frees me from being absorbed with checking out my value. If "who I am" is someone truly worthwhile, then I can stop worrying about myself and instead start thinking about others. I can even start thinking about God. Finally I can begin noticing somebody besides me.

We all need to change from self-centered to other-centered, from self-centered to God-centered. Such a shift warms God's heart and

gifts our hearts as well. We live in the presence of a God who says
He wants above all for us to love Him and love others, the exact
opposite of the way most of us live our lives.

Instead of loving others, all too often we treat them like pieces
of furniture – someone we're careful not to trip over but not
someone we actually relate to. Think back to the last time you were
standing with nine other people in front of the mirror in an airport
restroom. I don't know about guys' restrooms, but in women's
restrooms, everyone is washing her own hands and checking out
her own hair, ignoring every other woman there unless her suitcase
blocks you from the sink.

We're much more skilled at focusing on ourselves than on others;
each one of us has been doing it for years. Take me, for example.
Something inside me hates to step out of the spotlight. When
I walk into a party, I'm not concerned about whether the other
people look good; I'm concerned about whether I look good. When
I walk by those shiny department store windows, I'd much rather
look at my reflection than at the mannequins wearing sequins. You
may get spinach in your teeth during lunch, but when I glance at
you my interest instantly shifts to whether I have any spinach in my
own teeth. You get my point.

So we're going to consider who we are, but not to get stuck on
ourselves. Not at all. The whole point of knowing our identity is to
be free from our preoccupation with self and able to get on with the
real business of life: love.

And what is love? Love is receptivity. Think of it as unconditionally
opening yourself to others and welcoming them into your heart.
We're to keep the door of our heart open, not only to God but

also to people, even to that little old lady in line ahead of us at the supermarket slowly searching through her purse for a seven-cent soap coupon. We're to accept her, not as an object but as a person. But we can't do that until we take our attention off ourselves (our inconvenience, our frustration) and turn our attention to her (her embarrassment, her frustration).

Love requires that we notice *her*; we already know how to notice ourselves. We don't need to learn who we are so we can *increase* our self-absorption; we need to learn who we are so we can get *over* our self-absorption. And we won't do that until we're sure of who we are in God's eyes. *The point of knowing who I am in Christ isn't to then live a more self-centered life, it's to get over myself and love God and others.*

You may already know the Lord of the Bible. You may be in the process of being drawn to Him. Either way, God has some remarkable words for you. He knows who you are. He's certain of your worth. And He wants you to be as sure of it as He is.

If you're unsure about your identity, if you long to know without a doubt that you are someone of great value, if you're interested in what the God of the Bible has to say about who you are, if you're sick of your self-centeredness – please, read on.

3
Identity Problems

A lot of people wish they were different than they are. I don't mean losing fifteen pounds, I mean having a different identity, a different self – inside. I was sitting in Starbucks the other day, writing, when a man approached the woman next to me. "You don't happen to be Kim, do you?" "No, I'm sorry," she said. And the stranger walked away. She was sorry because she was Julie ... and he was looking for Kim. The scene reminded me of Woody Allen's lament: "My only regret in life is that I'm not someone else." Has that regret ever crossed your mind? The popular guys at school.

Some of us suffer (and we really do suffer) from "low self-esteem." Some of us are totally confident – until life pulls the carpet out from under us, and our sense of worth collapses. Either way, the majority of us remain ignorant of our value. We have identity problems.

Fixing Ourselves Up

When faced with identity problems, most of us react by trying to make ourselves "better people." *I'll stop being late. Lose a few pounds. Be pleasant to lagging drivers. Keep my temper. Live up to my New Year's resolutions.*

Good luck.

Self-help books support our attempts to fix ourselves up. They also ignore the high failure rate of such efforts. These wildly popular books rest on the misguided premise that we actually are able to improve ourselves. As I just said, good luck. Take a look at the historical evidence: you've been trying to improve yourself for years with minimal success.

The best thing I've done is humbled myself and asked God to grow me.

Not only do our attempts to rid ourselves of flaws assume we have the ability to do so – a rather arrogant assumption – but such efforts amount to one more form of self-absorption. All this attention to self leaves us with little time or inclination to focus on anybody else. We make other people wait in line while we attempt to get ourselves together.

Self-help books aren't the only evidence of our identity problems. Personal insecurity drives huge numbers into therapy. Having a shrink has become a modern necessity. But, like self-help books, most therapy assumes we have the ability to change ourselves into better people. We don't. Only God can change us. Self-effort can't resolve self-doubt.

Our doubts about self, specifically about our worth, at a minimum give us moments of discomfort. At their worst, they generate a deep anxiety, sometimes even a terror, that another's penetrating glance will bring us shame. Our fear of exposure causes us to expend unbelievable amounts of time and effort trying to hide.

HIDING EXPOSED

Hiding has been going on for a long time. As Adam and Eve discovered, fig leaves failed to distract God from their sin *(Genesis 3:7-11)*. Our efforts at hiding (with our fig-leaf styled masks) are equally ineffective in turning others' eyes away from our inner mess. Hiding doesn't work.

You may protest: "I don't hide! Faking it isn't my style." Think again. Have you ever feigned interest when you were truly bored? Worked long hours to impress your boss with a zeal you know is fake? Performed center-stage at a party to acquire friends, or at least attention? Shifted your tongue into overdrive after your first words fell flat? Focused attention on your successes to distract even your own eyes from that nagging sense of inner emptiness? These are fig leaves, self-styled masks. And they are yours.

Trying to distract others from noticing "the real me" takes a lot of work. It wears us out. The effort, of course, seems well worth it, considering the alternative – being clearly seen, and rejected. Our desire to look good and our fear of being seen are powerful motivators. Unfortunately, they motivate hypocrisy: we become actors on a public stage who hope others will notice our act and ignore our flawed selves.

Others seldom comment on our phoniness when they see it. (After all, we don't comment on theirs.) The lack of feedback leads us to think we've pulled it off. *Yes! I can fool others!* So we continue our charade with fervor. These roles we create become precious to us, and we cling to them like life preservers.

CLINGING TO A ROLE

I was in my late twenties, a married career woman, independent
and competent, and my role stroked my ego nicely. My husband
and I started planning a family and soon welcomed our long
anticipated firstborn into the world. So far, so good.

When I took our newborn for the first visit to the pediatrician, a
small problem developed. The doctor walked in, smiled, and said
"Hi, Mom." Big mistake. Ever quick on the draw, I said "Lynne!
My name is Lynne!" as I put a strangle hold on his neck. (Actually,
it didn't go that far … I didn't attack him physically. Let's just say
my response was a bit overdone.)

Why the big reaction? Because I'd had my role grabbed right out
from under my feet. It wasn't about not wanting to mother. Not at
all. I wanted to mother, but I wasn't about to let go of the career-
woman identity I had so carefully forged. My shallow sense of
worth was mine, and no doctor was going to mess with it. He said
"Hi, Mom!" And I panicked. I thought I was going to lose my
carefully constructed "me."

I had no idea my role had become so precious to me until I over-
reacted to the pediatrician. I had come to depend on my career
competence to look good, both in others' eyes as well as in my own.
My role was a mask I used to define my identity. I still had no idea
that real value came from God; I thought I had to *create* it. And,
since I believed that worth could be lost, I thought I had to *protect*
it. My sense of self rested on a shaky foundation: it came from what
I did.

OTHER SLIPPERY CHOICES

My actions provided me with an identity – not a reliable one,
but an identity nonetheless. Action-based identity might be your

specialty, too. But don't limit yourself. If you can handle instability, you have a lot of other undependable choices: gaining self-esteem from what others think about you, boosting your ego by acquiring stuff, hanging around important people so you'll feel important too, perhaps trying to locate a valuable inner being through some form of meditation.

I gave Buddhist meditation a good try by the way. It relaxed me, but I was still a mess. I tried other things, too – Esalen encounter therapy groups, Universalist spiritual gatherings, hanging around with a free (some would say "loose") crowd. As you can probably guess all too easily, none of my efforts got rid of my fear of humiliation. I remained skittish around insightful people, tense lest my mask crack and reveal the loser behind it. I played the phantom in my own opera.

Such self-engineered attempts to gain a stable worthwhile identity all have a common problem: they aren't reliable. The information we gather to buoy up our worth keeps shifting on us, and as it shifts, so does our sense of self. How can we be sure we've done well? How do we ever know if we've done enough?

Where can we turn? We need a dependable basis for our identity that doesn't depend on our own efforts. Something real that can't disappear. A basis of worth that is immune to doubt. Not too many recognize God as the creator of our worth, and even fewer believe what He says about our innate splendor.

God says we delight Him. We think He's crazy. Our primary regret in life is that we're not someone else. We have a problem. Whether our problem with self is long standing or revealed suddenly through a crisis makes little difference. The solution is the same: we need to move beyond our definition of who we are

to God's definition of who we are. His description of our identity
must replace our skewed perceptions.

CLINGING TO THE ROCK

God's words about us aren't flimsy like Walter Mitty's fantasies.
Not at all. His message to us is rock-solid; He doesn't feed us
wishes or delusions – God describes reality. We can trust His words
because He's speaking from first-hand experience. Who knows us
better than the One who created us?

God tells us He has given us a worth which will never spoil or
fade away, an inner dignity that can't be punctured by exposure or
ridicule or a lost job or a nasty smile or a cold shoulder. The worth
with which God has shaped us won't disappear when we need it
most.

Our identity itself is as unchanging as rock. Our view of our
identity is less dependable. Our nagging doubts
about our value don't come from God; they come

*Our identity is
solid. Our view
of our identity
is less so.*

from listening to someone besides God – maybe to
other people we admire or maybe to those whispers
inside our own heads. Whatever. But any message
that leads us away from a sense of innate worth
doesn't come from God. And trusting such messages causes identity
problems.

Solving these identity problems requires a shift in focus: plugging
our ears to false messages and clinging instead to what God has to
say. I waited a long time before trying that solution, delaying not
so much out of ignorance as out of fear. Trusting God was my last
card, and I wasn't going to play it unless everything else failed.
Eventually I had to play that card and I gave myself to God – I

asked Jesus to take over my life. When I did, I found to my surprise that yielding to the Lord opened my eyes. I could finally see. I saw that nothing is more real than God, nothing is more trustworthy than His words, and no role I can manufacture has more value than the person He created me to be.

What does God have to say about our identity? Quite a lot. He starts by describing Himself.

PART II
Real Worth
and
Pseudoworth

PART II OVERVIEW
REAL WORTH AND PSEUDOWORTH

An early Russian cosmonaut, after announcing that he couldn't see God in the heavens, gloatingly stated his fallacious conclusion: God must not exist! Too bad the cosmonaut relied on his skeptical eyes.

We buy into a similar fallacy about our worth. We look for visible evidence of our value (possessions, successes, youth, beauty), find a lot of contradictory evidence, and conclude that our self-worth is more defective than our flabby abs.

But what if our value isn't tied to the visible? What if we (the person inside) can't be seen, but can be known? What if value, though not visible, is nonetheless real?

The second part of this book sets the worth God has given us side-by-side with the pseudoworth we manufacture on our own. Chapters 4-6 reveal three Biblical perspectives on who we are. Chapters 7-9 unmask the false selves we substitute for the self whom God has created.

Are you hungry for real worth?

4
Spirit, Wind, and Breath: Identity and God

We are so like God that we can't even begin to describe ourselves until we describe Him. We will never figure out who we are if we don't know who God is. And we will never find our own identity until we find His.

How do we learn who God is? We look at His stories, and we look at His name.

STORIES AND A NAME

God often uses a story to disclose Himself. If you've ever been to church, or even Sunday school, you've seen Him as a father caring for his family, as a mother cradling a weaned baby against her breast, as a shepherd guiding His flock towards home. These are all wonderful stories; they're all true, and each describes what God does.

But there's more to God than what He *does*. God also tells us who He *is* – He tells us about the being behind His activity. We see this clearly when Moses asks God His name. God doesn't answer Moses with a noun, like father or mother or shepherd. Instead God replies with a verb, and not an action verb but a verb of being. You might even call it a verb of identity. God tells Moses to call Him "I AM."[1] Why would God do this?

NAMES TELL THE TRUTH

In the Bible, names signify a person's deepest character; they describe the inside of a person; they reveal self. Examples abound. Look at Adam. After disobeying God, with death swirling around him, he names his wife "Eve." Eve means life. It seems like an inopportune time to choose such a positive name, but Adam knew what he was doing. He chose the name "Life" because God had promised him that from this woman Jesus the Life-Giver would descend.[2] Eve represents life, and Adam named her with exactly the right name.

The book of Ruth tells of a name change with a different twist. Ruth's mother-in-law, Naomi, (contrary to what you hear about most mothers-in-law) had a delightful personality. Naomi means delightful, but her delight didn't last. After the death of her husband and sons, Naomi asks to be called "Mara" – bitter – to reflect the harsh shift of her heart.[3]

God's name, like Eve's and Mara's, reveals His nature, the self behind all His activity. And God's name is not about what He *does*;

His name is about who He *is*. God names Himself "I AM." He has named Himself perfectly... and we don't have a clue what His name means. 'I AM." I am *what*? God's answer? "I am spirit."

GOD IS: A SPIRIT-LIKE BEING

God is spirit. Jesus pointedly makes that equation in John 4:24:

> **God is Spirit**, and those who worship Him must worship in Spirit and truth.

Jesus isn't announcing a new idea. At the very beginning of creation, long before Jesus speaks to His disciples, even before God speaks matter into existence, spirit and God have already been paired:

> *Genesis 1:2 And the earth was formless and void, and darkness was over the surface of the deep, and the **Spirit** of **God** was moving over the surface of the waters.*

In Genesis 1:2, *spirit* describes God's presence, while in John 4:24, *spirit* describes God Himself. God plainly says He's a spirit-like being, but what is His point? The word *spirit* sounds so otherworldly that it's difficult to understand what God is getting at. We want a more tangible description of God, something less vague.

We solve our problem by going back to the meaning of spirit in the Bible. In both the Old and the New Testaments, the word used for spirit also suggests wind and breath.[4] This helps; it helps considerably. We may be unable to grasp the meaning of spirit, but we do have a lot of experience with wind and breath. And both wind and breath give us clues, not only about the meaning of spirit but also about the nature of our spirit-wind-breath-like God. Notice that I said clues, not a direct view. After all, as you know, wind and breath are invisible. So is God.

God is mysterious as spirit yet familiar as wind. What do we know about wind?

GOD IS: A WIND-LIKE BEING

Could you tell if the wind was blowing when you walked out to fetch your newspaper this morning? Yes? How? For starters, you saw your want-ads section following the neighbor's trash can down the street. Of course, you couldn't actually see the wind itself, but its effect made you sure it was there – sure enough, perhaps, to throw a few choice words in its direction.

Your neighbor won't think you're crazy for yelling those words at something he can't see. He may find you irritating, especially if you woke him up, but he won't think you've lost your mind. You were responding to a thing invisible, yet obviously present. A thing unseen, yet still knowable.

Wind can be powerful (strong enough to lean against), gentle (slightly lifting the edge of the curtain), or anything in between. We can't draw a picture of the wind – it doesn't have any edges. We certainly can't control it or predict it; on the contrary, wind keeps surprising us with the unexpected. Will we feel a sudden gust? Where will it come from? Who knows?!

Wind is invisible but obviously present, unseen, but still knowable. So is God.

I'm not saying that God *is* the wind. But He is *like* it: invisible, yet obviously present; unseen, yet still knowable; strong enough to lean on; gentle enough to comfort us; unpredictable enough to keep surprising us; and definitely not under our control. He's a "wind-like" being.

GOD IS: A BREATH-LIKE BEING

God is also a "breath-like" being. Breath, like wind and spirit, escapes our vision. On a cold day, we might say, "I can see my breath!" But we're really seeing only the condensation of water molecules: the result of breath, not breath itself. Breath, like wind and spirit, moves. Like them, it has no discernible shape. And one more thing – breath is necessary for life.

Breath is necessary for life. As I looked at the words I'd written I startled. I'd been thinking about inhaling and exhaling, regular breathing, the kind that keeps us walking around. Then another reality broke the surface: I'm not talking about our breath, I'm talking about God's. Our breath only keeps our body alive; His breath makes *us* alive. This is profound. It's miracle. Our breath is merely physical. God's breath is spiritual; it wafts deep within us, touching us with the kind of life that transforms who we are.

> *Human breath, though invisible, keeps bodies alive. God's breath, also invisible keeps self alive.*

But we're getting ahead of ourselves – before God breathes into us, He breathes into Adam. Adam's story precedes our own. We'll never understand how God brings life to us until we watch Him bring life to Adam. That ancient scene will surprise you: Adam comes to life when God breathes into mud.

NOTES
CHAPTER 4 – SPIRIT, WIND, AND BREATH:
IDENTITY AND GOD

1. In Exodus 3:14-15 Moses calls God *Yahweh*, a Hebrew word
    which means "He is," God calls Himself "I AM," the same
    name that Jesus calls Himself in John 8:58.

2. *Genesis 3:20 Now the man called his wife's name Eve, because she
    was the mother of all the living.*

3. *Ruth 1:19 So they both went until they came to Bethlehem. And
    it came about when they had come to Bethlehem, that all the city
    was stirred because of them, and the women said, "Is this Naomi?"
    20 And she said to them, "Do not call me Naomi; call me Mara,
    for the Almighty has dealt very bitterly with me. 21 I went out
    full, but the LORD has brought me back empty. Why do you call
    me Naomi, since the LORD has witnessed against me and the
    Almighty has afflicted me?"*

4. In the Old Testament the English word *spirit* generally
    translates the Hebrew word *ruach*. In the New Testament *spirit*
    generally translates the Greek word *pneuma*. Our English word
    for spirit is a bit narrow, since both *ruach* and *pneuma* connote
    not only what we think of as spirit, but also imply wind and
    breath. When we translate *ruach* or *pneuma* into English, we
    usually choose a single English word – spirit or wind or breath
    – even though no single English word quite matches the three-
    fold scope of the original Hebrew and Greek words.

5
Blowing into Mud Pies: Identity and Adam

I've made pies from all kinds of things: rhubarb, mincemeat, even mud. Rhubarb is my favorite. Sometimes I've blown a cooling breath over my forkful of rhubarb before popping it into my mouth. But no breath of mine ever caused my rhubarb to spring to life and move slowly across the tabletop. My breath doesn't bring the inanimate to life. God's does.

God starts mankind with a mud pie. He takes a bushel full of dirt (perhaps more – Adam may have been a big guy), molds it into the masculine form we all recognize, blows into His earthen lump, and

the mud springs to life! If we were standing nearby we could have
seen it happen. Earth + Breath becomes Adam.

The transition from mud to Adam goes far beyond a bodily

> *Adam's self is as
> invisible as the God
> after whom he is
> patterned.*

event. Adam comes alive not just physically but
personally. Our spirit-wind-breath-like God exhales
His spirit-wind-breath-like image into Adam and
so makes Adam like Himself. Adam's inner self is
as invisible as the God after whom he is patterned.
The image and likeness of God can't be seen.

GOD'S IMAGE AND LIKENESS

The very first time He talks about mankind God links our breath-
like essence with His own. He uses the words *image* and *likeness* to
do so:

> *Genesis 1:26 Then God said, "Let Us make mankind in Our*
> ***image****, according to Our **likeness**; and let them rule over the fish*
> *of the sea and over the birds of the sky and over the cattle and*
> *over all the earth, and over every creeping thing that creeps on the*
> *earth." 27 God created man in His own **image**, in the **image** of*
> *God He created him; male and female He created them.*

Image and *likeness*. These two words tell us we resemble God. Adam
does, Eve does, and so does every man and woman. Each of us and
all of us are made in the image and likeness of God.

THE IMAGE OF GEORGE

Now be careful with this idea of being like God – don't start
thinking that you duplicate God. Neither image nor likeness
implies duplication.[1] God doesn't copy and paste Himself; He
doesn't clone Himself. And when God makes Adam, He doesn't
make another God.

Think of it this way: an image or likeness can do no more than remind us of the original, just like the picture of George Washington on a dollar bill reminds us of George. Everyone knows that the picture isn't the real George – it just calls George to mind. Adam isn't the real God, but he does call God to mind.

How does God give Adam this resemblance to Himself? Look at the details of the event.

GOD'S BREATH AND ADAM'S SELF

In Genesis 2:7, we read about Adam's first moments:

> *Then the Lord **God** formed man² of dust from the ground, and **breathed** into his **nostrils** the **breath** of **life**; and man² became a **living being**.*

On the surface it looks straightforward enough: God forms the man, Adam, and brings him to life. But the words God uses to describe this event deserve more than a quick read. Five of the words in this verse refer to breath and two others imply breath. Add them up. Seven times God calls our attention to breath. One little verse. Seven references to breath. The breath-like God is making a breath-like Adam. Seven repetitions. We're intended to notice.

Look at the five explicit references to breath: *God, breathed, nostrils, breath,* and *being.* We've already seen *God* use the spirit-wind-breath words from Genesis 1:2 and John 4:24 to connect Himself with breath. Now we read that this breath-like God *breathed* a sustained, strong stream of air into the man's *nostrils* (the place where Adam breathes). The miracle continues. A particular short puff of air, a *breath,* turns Adam into a living *being.* How does *being* relate to breathing? *Being* comes from a word that means "to take a breath."

Now look at the two places where breath is implied: the breath of *life*, and a *living* being. This connection may not seem so clear – how does life imply breath? You may not have thought about it, but you already assume a connection between the two: only living things breathe.

Those of us who have cared for infants remember checking on the sleeping babies to make sure they were okay. We did it by watching to see if their little chests were moving up and down. *Are they breathing? Oh, yes, there, I see it; they're alive; they're fine.* On the other end of a lifespan, we know that death has occurred when breathing ceases.

God often uses physical analogies to point to spiritual truths, and He's doing so here with life and breath. Breath and life come, and go, together. Everyone makes that connection, including God. His two references to life remind us of breath.

Breath, breath, breath, breath, breath, life, life. One idea, seven repetitions. Repetition brings emphasis, and God makes sure we don't miss His meaning: *The man is like Me! My breath defines him. Look, I'm using My breath to make him in My image!*

> Adam, like God, is a breath-like being.

Take a moment and think about what all this means. By connecting Himself to spirit, wind, and breath, God has revealed that He's that kind of being. Genesis 2:7 tells us that Adam is that kind of being too. Adam bears God's image because he's brought to life by God's breath. (As we'll see later, so are we.)

If we open our hearts we still can sense this resemblance to God, though sometimes dimly, in each other. At times of unabashed receptivity, we may even sense His likeness in ourselves. We all, no matter how worn or warped or torn, bear the mark of our spirit-wind-breath-like God. Each of us ought to call God to mind. That rarely happens. We tend to identify with less lofty things.

NOTES

CHAPTER 5 – BLOWING INTO MUD PIES:
IDENTITY AND ADAM

1. *Image* translates the Hebrew word *tselem* which means image, form, or resemblance. Likeness translates the Hebrew word *demut* which means a likeness or resemblance. Both words suggest a pattern or model of the original – like it but not identical to it. Neither *tselem* nor *demut* imply that the real thing has been reproduced.

2. Literally, "the man," i.e. Adam.

6

Our Invisible Self: Identity and Us

What identifies us? According to the clerk at the drugstore, it's our driver's license. The clerk isn't thinking biblically; he just wants to make sure we haven't stolen the credit card we're using. If we do think biblically, though, the real question isn't *what* identifies us, but *who* identifies us. Adam, of course, didn't have a driver's license, but Adam was credentialed by the God who exhaled him into existence. Adam was God's type.

We're God's type too.

If we could fill in our entire genealogy, we'd eventually get back to our first ancestor, not Adam but God. While none of us duplicates God, every one of us bears a family resemblance to Him. You might say we all have the family nose.

The Scope of God's Image

God patterns every one of us after Himself. Everybody. Anybody. Male and female, you and me, that cousin we enjoy and the other one we can't stand. Look at the scope of our likeness to God:

> *Genesis 1:26 Then God said, "Let Us make **mankind** in Our image, according to Our likeness; and let **them** rule over the fish of the sea and over the birds of the sky and over the cattle and over all the earth, and over every creeping thing that creeps on the earth. 27 And God created **man** in His own image, in the image of God He created **him**; **male and female** He created **them**.*

The language is all-inclusive. God connects his image to *mankind* – that means everybody. He pairs Himself with *them* (twice) and with *man* and with *him* and with *male and female*. They all, male and female – we all, male and female – are made in God's image. He has made us spirit-wind-breath-like beings like Himself. Every one of us exists in the likeness of our invisible God.

The Problem with Invisibility

God's invisibility seems obvious, interesting, and irrelevant to the issue at hand: trying to figure out who we are. But it's not irrelevant at all. If we inside are made in the image of a God who can't be seen, that means that we inside can't be seen either. Self, like God, is invisible to our eyes. You'd almost think we're not there – until we remember that self (like God) is present but not physical and that self (like God) is invisible yet altogether real.

Self can't be seen.

Self is invisible. Great. We're already worried about our worth; now we find we can't even get visible evidence of our value. This "invisible-me" notion doesn't look very promising, especially since we routinely use what we see to define who we are.

You may not think you spend much time looking for observable signs of your status. Perhaps you don't, but that's unlikely. With concrete signals of worth so available and so familiar, we gravitate to them and think nothing of it. We need to be more cautious – visible status symbols have serious drawbacks. Besides their inability to represent an invisible self, they jolt us with their inconsistency and disappoint us with their transitory nature.

> *The visible can't make you valuable.*

Depending on the inconsistent doesn't work

Visible signs of success – jobs, money, praise from others, power – lure us with an empty promise, "I'll make you valuable!" Don't get your hopes up. The promise ought to read, "I'll make you valuable ... unless you fail."

It's impossible to predict the outcome of our efforts. Have you ever expected praise and been treated like a fool? Worked hard and lost a job? Prepared carefully and bombed a presentation? Thought you knew your material and had your ignorance exposed? The world may applaud our output and later spit on it; its feedback changes faster than the color of a chameleon. Efforts to boost our egos fail us because the responses we get are so inconsistent. We need something more dependable.

Depending on the temporary doesn't work

The visible not only sends inconsistent messages; it also doesn't last. Beauty fades. Intellect wanes. A multi-million dollar athlete, old at

age 30, loses the crowd as his abilities decline. Visible signs of worth
are always temporary.

Everything we can now see is temporary. Paul spells out this truth
clearly. In the midst of visibly harsh circumstances, he urges the
Corinthians to look with him beyond their circumstances. He does
so to keep them from being falsely swayed by what they see.

> *2 Corinthians 4:18 while we look not at the things which are seen,
> but at the things which are not seen;* **for the things which are
> seen are temporal,** *but the things which are not seen are eternal.*

He's asking them to focus not on what they could see but on what
would endure. Most of us gloss right over these words and never
consider that God might be right: only the invisible – the spiritual
– lasts.

Fear of fading

I used to worry about heaven. Specifically, I worried that I'd get
bored. After years of nothing but glory, wouldn't glory lose its
appeal? Surely unending pleasure would slowly fade into banality.
I changed my mind when I read that the treasures of heaven don't
fade away.[1] They don't die off or disappear or grow stale. In a realm
where everything stays fresh, boredom is impossible. I should
have worried instead about the material realm – everything there
eventually does fade into nothingness.

I mention my fear of fading because it directly applies to self-worth.
What if our sense of worth slips away from us because we base it on
something that *always* slips away? If Paul is right about what lasts,
then basing our worth on what we can see will sink our self-esteem
quicker than a hike through quicksand. Paul is right. Finding a
worth that lasts requires us to look beyond the material to the
spiritual world.

Many of us are uncomfortable taking that step. Depending on the spiritual makes us uneasy. Spiritual information (though, of course, *true*) seems far removed from everyday issues like establishing our worth. It appears so otherworldly. We wonder if the spiritual has any practical uses in the world in which we live.

MISTRUST AND FEAR

Our preference for that which can be seen stems from our mistrust of the unseen. When we face the fact that an invisible God has formed us in His invisible image, we begin to whine: *What good is an invisible self? I need concrete evidence of my worth — not some platitudes about resembling an invisible God. I want data I can verify. Give me something solid.*

As wrong as my grandma

My dad once said that my grandma would rather be positive than right. She isn't the only one. We live our lives certain that the seen is more dependable than the unseen, positive about our opinion, and as wrong as my grandma. Part of our disagreement with God comes from the alluring familiarity of the visible world. Part comes from our rebellious commitment to depend on our own resources – our physical senses – rather than on the words of our God. And part comes from fear. I know about fear.

I would never join a trapeze act. Never. That moment in midair, desperate for the next trapeze to arrive, wondering if I can grab its bar with my sweaty palms ... I would never do it. Fear of losing my grip and hurtling towards the concrete floor would squelch any attempt to cross over to the tiny platform on the other side. If someone stuck me on a trapeze I'd just swing back and forth with a death grip on its bar until someone mercifully lowered it to the ground and I could go home.

We fear another kind of death, this one not physical but personal. Our fear of worthlessness and its consequences – rejection, scorn, being alone – causes us to cling tenaciously to our familiar strategies for earning acceptance and managing relational security. Desperate to reassure our hearts, we keep a death grip on any evidence of our value, however miniscule. We search for a "material me."

THE SEARCH FOR A MATERIAL ME

I know in my head that visible things can't tell me about my invisible self, and most of the time in my heart I even believe it. Still, I find it incredibly easy to fall into the visible trap – there are so many enticing choices. I love when people laugh at my jokes; it definitely ups my self-esteem. So does looking good or at least thinking I do. If I'm honest with myself, I don't exercise because I like it; I exercise because I enjoy compliments: "You look really good for your age."

Things I own boost my ego too. I just bought a new sweater, gorgeous color, great fit, and when I wear it I actually feel better about myself. This is crazy. And commonplace.

Erroneous ego boosts

We notice what we have, what we do, and what others think of us, and use all three to define who we are. We're in error, for these visible things will never reveal an invisible self. Our misplaced focus forms a formidable barrier to knowing our true identity. Let me say it again: self can't be seen.

While we can see a lot of things, none of them evidence our inner beauty. We can see the physical body that contains us, but we can't see the self inside that container. We can see things we have, like our watch, but watches are clearly just possessions, not selves.

We can see the effects of self-activity, but we can't see self itself; neither God nor His image can be seen with our eyes.

We can locate what's on the outside of our body: our fingernails, our bellybutton, even our nose if we look cross-eyed. A surgeon can locate the organs inside the body. But how do we locate a self? Unlike a spleen, a self has no edges – it doesn't even have a shape. Unlike a stomach, self isn't somewhere in us; it *is* us.

Self is not only invisible; it's inaudible, unsmellable, untasteable, and untouchable. Self, like God, is present, but not physical. You'll need to undo all those habits of defining yourself by what you can physically perceive.

> *Self is present, but not physical. Self is invisible, yet altogether real.*

BEHIND THE VISIBLE

A brief thought about our efforts to find a tangible self might bring a smile, but a more lengthy survey should sadden us. Searching for a material "me" is a waste of time, a useless effort. God doesn't identify us with the material world; the Invisible One identifies us with Himself. *Self can't be seen.* Mumble these words until they're written on your heart.

Now don't get discouraged and don't give up, because invisible doesn't mean unknowable. While we can't see God, we can still comprehend something of His existence and the exquisiteness of His character. Self is like God. Neither can be seen, but both can be known, and known in all their exquisite glory.

DEFINING WHO WE AREN'T

But let's slow down. We're getting ahead of ourselves. Before we can comprehend inner glory, we must differentiate our real self from three common surrogate selves: possessions, activity, and the input from others. Our spirit-like identity is separate from what we have, separate from what we do, and separate from what others have or do or think. It's crucial to distinguish these self-substitutes from self.

Before we can define who we are, we must define who we aren't.

NOTES

CHAPTER 6 – IMAGE AND SELF: IDENTITY AND US

1. *1 Peter 1:3 Blessed be the God and Father of our Lord Jesus Christ, who according to His great mercy has caused us to be born again to a living hope through the resurrection of Jesus Christ from the dead, 4 to obtain an inheritance which is imperishable and undefiled **and will not fade away**, reserved in heaven for you.*

·

7
Differentiating Self from Stuff

Blind to reality. I've watched it first-hand.

I walk into our living room at dusk and startle at the tall shadow.
I thought I was alone! Who's standing there? A second look corrects
my mistake. *Wait. It's only the wood stove, disguised as a stranger.* Not
a real stranger, just an illusion. I've been scammed (again) by
a shadow.

I'm not the only one who stumbles over false realities; your eyes
trick you too. Daydreams and fantasies, illusions and delusions
repeatedly intrude into our physical and mental worlds. Distortions
of spiritual reality, like false views of self, are even more widespread.

SELF-DELUSIONS

We're delusional, and I do mean delusional, about our identity. In the average delusion people react to something that's *not* there. They act like little kids running to their mom at two in the morning screaming about imaginary spiders under their bed sheets. Self-delusions are different. With self-delusions we fail to react to something that *is* there – our invisible self.

Self-delusions spring to life when we trust our eyes to show us who we are. Eyes can check out wood stoves, but they can't check out selves. Adam's story (chapter 5) has just taught us that self can't be seen, but we don't believe God's words.

We think self can be seen, so, naturally, we look at the things we *can* see to tell us who we are, things like our possessions. Other people support our error – they also evaluate us by the stuff we have. (It's not surprising. We do the same to them.) This fallacy that stuff defines self looks true, in great measure because so many voices support it. We buy right into the idea that what we have changes who we are.

Our focus on visible stuff makes God's truth murky and blinds us to our real identity. We develop spiritual cataracts, deeply ingrained (and erroneous) beliefs that block an accurate assessment of self. Our false beliefs veil reality, forcing us to work hard to peer through their camouflage. Only a careful stare differentiates stoves from strangers. It takes an even more penetrating gaze to differentiate self from self-substitutes like our possessions. Although we often identify with stuff, who we are is quite different from what we possess.

IDENTIFYING WITH OUR POSSESSIONS

Behind all that we have is us. Stuff is not self. We're all born naked, known as little individuals long before we accumulate any belongings. Self is there before stuff even enters the picture. Look again at Adam's creation in Genesis 2:7.

> *Then the Lord God formed man of dust from the ground, and breathed into his nostrils the breath of life; and man **became** a living being.*

Read God's words carefully: man became a living being. Became, not had. Adam doesn't have anything, no clothes, no car, no mortgage. Adam doesn't even have a self; he becomes a self. Genesis 2:7 makes it impossible to confuse self with possessions. Whatever you call it – self, being, core, essence, identity, worth – it is not *his*, it is *him*.

Possessions don't shape Adam's identity. That much is clear. But the clarity of Adam's identity eludes us when we try to figure out our own identity. As I've just said, we often derive self-worth from our possessions; we confuse what we have with who we are.

Go ahead and argue with me. Maybe you don't define your self by your stuff. Maybe. Yet have you ever noticed your sense of worth inflating (just a bit) when you get some thing you value? Something simple like a great tan, or more prestigious like a promotion to manager, or perhaps even a car with eyeballs. Join the crowd.

Even when we know the shallowness of this lie, we still struggle not to identify with our possessions. Who doesn't feel more important when they're connected to assets (or people) they prize? There's a catch, of course, a flip side. We also feel less valuable when we're associated with something, or someone, we find boring or perhaps embarrassing. (Who *were* you talking with at that party when you felt an urge to join a different conversation?)

A lot of people confuse self with stuff. Stuff like a motorcycle.

CONFUSING SELF WITH A HARLEY

Harleys are wonderful. To a lot of people, like me, even the sound of their engine is a turn-on. I love to look at these bikes. So does my friend Ted. One day while standing around with a group of people admiring a Harley, Ted got intrigued by the behavior of its owner who had both a Harley and an identity problem.

The owner would stand next to his bike, drinking in the group's admiration, but feeling a little jealous that they were noticing the bike and not him. He didn't want to share the limelight with his Harley, so he'd move away from the bike, hoping the attention would follow him. But everybody kept looking at the Harley. So he'd move back next to the bike and into their attention. Then move away and end up ignored. Back and forth. Again and again. What a sad dance. The Harley gave him a fleeting sense of worth, but nothing that lasted. He knew that all that love was going to the Harley and not to him.

The Harley guy used something visible to feel valuable and ended up frustrated. He obviously wanted to be somebody without depending on his bike, but couldn't think of an alternative to his sad dance. His Harley proved unreliable, at least as a source of self-worth. Using what he *had* to define who he *was* left him empty; his tactic sucked the self-esteem right out of him. My friend Ted told the story to point this out. (I wonder if Ted had a Harley. I forgot to ask.)

Don't blame motorcycles. I do the same thing with my car. I drive a little silver sport convertible; it matches my hair. When I'm driving around with the top down, hair flying in the wind, I sometimes play, just a little of course, with self-adoration. I actually expect the person driving next to me to look over and yell, "Hey! Go Babe!" Now I'm sixty-some years old, so this hasn't happened in awhile, but old patterns die hard. Uh oh. Wrong basis for self-esteem.

Having a snazzy sport car does not make me a different person. Neither would having a clunker.

HARLEYS AREN'T THE WHOLE PICTURE

It's pretty easy to differentiate self from external possessions, but what about our bodies? Do they define who we are? Not at all.

Let me explain. Right now I'm wearing a ring. Obviously the ring is not me. But how about the finger on which my ring rests? Say you were to suddenly chop off my finger, I'd lose a body part and I'd be very upset with you – and I'd still be me. The finger is mine, a mere possession, but it's not me. If you kept on chopping – arm, leg, second arm, second leg – eventually my body would die, but at no time in the process would I cease to be me. I am not my body. My body is only something I have, a mere container in which I live. It's *mine* but it's not *me*.

Visible, physical things like our bodies don't define us, but what about our minds? Who would question that our minds define us? Well, I would. Our minds can't establish who we are. We *have* minds – that means they are *ours*, but are not *us*.

Perhaps you have an exquisite gift of analysis, and you've just answered a question brilliantly. Now there is joy in an apt answer;

doing something well is a lot of fun. But apt (or inept) replies don't make you a better (or a worse) person.

Take another example. Suppose you go into a coma. If I come visit you in the hospital, I'll still greet you by name. Even if you don't respond to my voice, I'll still know that you are you.

What if I enter the last stages of Alzheimer's disease? My thinking will be confused and sparse, my emotions inappropriate or absent, my ability to process and choose greatly diminished. But even though my thoughts, emotions, and choices are so distorted, when you come by to see me you'll still know who I am. A mind lost, or markedly lessened, seems like a lost self, but that's not true. I'm hidden, but I've not disappeared.

Self doesn't disappear even when we're six-feet-under. Whose name will appear on our tombstone? Ours. When we meet God, will He know our name? Of course.

Stuff is not self. Not our car, our house, our brawn, or our brain. Not our job, our family, or our friends. They may be *ours*, but they're not *us*.

Our speech is revealing. We correctly say, "my car, my body, my mind, my soul, my spirit." Those words are fine. No problem. But we'll have a problem if we try to wrap our tongue around the phrase "my me" – it just doesn't compute. What is mine can't be me.

Stuff is not self. What is mine can't be me.

How about the phrase "my self"? As in, I'm going to improve *myself*. I don't like *myself*. What am I going to do with *myself*? I'm going to check *myself* out. The phrase is so common we fail to notice its inherent contradiction. We don't *have* a self; we *are* a self.

Failing to distinguish self from possessions feeds our fear of loss and its companions, hoarding and coveting. How so? Think about it. Possessions aren't noted for their permanence. Cars rust, houses burn, bodies wrinkle up and sag. Losses – socks, teeth, jobs, and health – abound. Stuff can't provide a secure sense of worth because it keeps disappearing. Relying on undependable stuff to define a dependable self can lead to a lot of anxiety.

Depending on stuff to define self also sets us up to hoard the possessions we have and covet those we don't. A lot of us accumulate beyond what makes sense, or hang onto things beyond their time. (Of course, if identity really is based on our stuff – IF – then we'd be smart to accumulate all we can and hang on tightly to everything we have.)

Naturally, possessions may serve other purposes. Stuff may bring a false sense of safety, providing comfort rather than status. It may provide a way to feel in touch with past relationships or past times. Acquisitions may (at least temporarily) satisfy a sense of entitlement to the "good life." Our motivations vary widely.

But what concerns me here is our use of stuff to get a sense of self-worth. Are we that blind to the inherent worth of our God-imaged self? Apparently so, because we keep using things as ephemeral as the stuff we have to try and get the worth God has already given us. Don't ever forget it: stuff is not self.

Neither is activity.

8

Differentiating Self from Activity

Beyond differentiating self from stuff, there's a second distinction we need to make: differentiating who we are from what we do. Have you ever defined your identity by your activity? Probably. Confusing self with activity happens as often as confusing self with stuff.

Gaining success or falling on our face, striving harder or acting the slacker – none of these change who we are. Nothing we do can change self, for better or for worse. Self-effort is simply not the same as self; we aren't defined by our deeds any more than we are by our possessions. Identity is not activity.

Look one more time at Genesis 2:7, this time scanning for who is doing what:

> Then the **Lord God** formed man of dust from the ground, and breathed into his nostrils the breath of life; and man became a living being.

Who is active during the man's creation? Certainly not Adam – the only one doing anything is God. Adam simply lies there in a lump while God shapes the soil and blows into it. The result of God's activity is awesome, and Adam's contribution is zero. God does everything. Adam becomes a living being without lifting a finger. (Lifting his finger comes later, but that's Michelangelo's version, not God's.) Adam's identity is a God's gift to him, not something Adam accomplishes.

Remember my encounter with the pediatrician, and the "Hi Mom" which yanked away my flimsy sense of worth? You may be glad to know I recovered quickly; I didn't take long to get over the shock. Deftly I replaced career-activity with mothering-activity, and career-based worth with mothering-based worth. Different choice but the same mistake.

I poured myself into being a good mom, an admirable goal but not a sound basis for worth. I hadn't yet learned that striving doesn't improve self. You may not have learned that either.

Learning to differentiate between self and activity takes some time. I'm still working at it. I recently glanced in the mirror and noticed that I was looking particularly disheveled and, well, old. I started to think about growing old and all the things I might lose, like being coherent or coordinated or capable of finding my way home. There

I was, looking in the mirror fixating on what I wouldn't be able to do. I found the whole thing very depressing. And also based on a lie. I don't create my value: God creates my value. Though getting a bit long in tooth, I remain forever an image bearer of God. As with Adam, God's activity defines me, not my own.

Our belief that our activity defines us isn't conjured up all by ourselves – Mom and Dad help. "Look what you did! What a great little girl you are!" The message, though its huge ramifications are likely unintended, still stamps itself on our psyche: *You are what you do*. Of course it's not all on our parents' shoulders; many others make well-meaning, yet significant, contributions to our misguided ideas about self.

I still remember the picture of a carrot I colored in nursery school – every orange stroke totally within the lines. I got to show it off; I felt great. Though only three, clearly I was special. Other achievements followed, from good report cards to doing a fine job at work. But mixed in with my success were my failures, and mixed in with my sense of being special was the shame I felt each time I fell short.

You've probably figured out by now that striving for status has been one of my specialties. Sometimes I feel almost guilty when I'm not doing anything – no, not guilty, more like anxious. Relaxing and feeling uneasy seem to occur together. Could I still be striving to define self by my activity? Could you?

9
Differentiating Self from Others

Others don't define us. Not by what they have; not by what they do, and not by what they think.

Someone else may have a lot more or less stuff than we do; their accomplishments may surpass or fall short of ours, but their status, whatever it is, has no impact on our identity. Neither does their opinion.

In real life, however, we often let other people impact our sense of self. We do so through a seemingly innocent practice: we compare ourselves with others.

Making Comparisons

The last time our family played a friendly board game, I had a great time, but later one of my kids told me they had no idea I was so competitive. I had played to win – decisively. My competitive (more like cutthroat) approach pleased me, until I found out I was being so obvious. I was embarrassed.

Nonetheless, winning lures me; I'll easily snap at that bait. Somehow I've learned the lie that besting others makes me more worthwhile than they are. This is absolutely not true.

I'm not the only one who makes this error. People compare themselves with others all the time, usually with the hope that they'll boost their own egos. Paul warns the Corinthians about this practice:

> *2 Corinthians 10:12 For we are not bold to class or* **compare**
> *ourselves with some of those who* **commend** *themselves; but when*
> *they measure themselves by themselves, and* **compare** *themselves*
> *with themselves, they are without understanding.*

The people who did this comparing were trying to feel good: they patted themselves on the back; they *commended* themselves. They fed their self-esteem by comparing themselves with others around them who, at least in their eyes, weren't as good as they were.

Paul refuses to mimic them. He says he's not bold enough to engage in their mind-game, and for good reason: comparing ourselves with others robs us of understanding. It really does.

Several false assumptions support our willingness to compare ourselves with others. We may assume that some people actually *are* better than others. Or perhaps we think that we have the ability to discern what has value without God's input, imagining ourselves fully qualified to differentiate what or who should be praised or scorned. We may also assume that other people are the standard against which we should measure ourselves. None of these assumptions are true.

We make another even more serious error. Comparing ourselves with others focuses our attention on people and causes us to neglect the only comparison that *will* bring us understanding: comparing ourselves with God. People aren't the standard; God is. Had the people in Corinth compared themselves with God they would have discovered that their righteousness fell far short of His.[1] If we compare ourselves with God we'll come to the same uncomfortable conclusion. Our resulting discomfort pushes us to look away from God and focus on people, hoping to get some more positive input. To that end, we notice what others have and do and use that information to define our worth.

In and of itself, noticing others doesn't get us into trouble. On the contrary, used rightly, noticing others allows us to love them. Our trouble comes when we use what we notice about others to compare ourselves with them. *Do you have more than I do? Are you better at this than I am?* More than. Better than. Less than. Worse than.

Comparing ourselves with other people trips us up. Instead of helping us, it leads us astray. We set ourselves side by side with others and decide which of us is better and which is worse. We judge them; we judge ourselves. And we end up deluded by either arrogance or shame. Comparing leads to pseudoworth – a deep misunderstanding of who we are.

NOTICING WHAT OTHERS HAVE

I recently heard about a study which discovered that having more money actually doesn't make people more happy. There's no correlation at all. For the people in the study the issue was not how *much* money they had but whether or not they had *more* money than the people around them. They compared themselves with others and felt rather elated.

You and I make comparisons too. We apologize when the dish we brought to a party doesn't look as appealing as the one our neighbor brought. We're embarrassed when our few extra pounds compare unfavorably with the weight of the person we're talking to. We decide that others' homes or cars or TV sets are better or worse than ours. Having a bad-hair day may be uncomfortable, but standing next to someone whose hair looks rattier than ours rapidly improves our mood.

Defining ourselves by what someone else has obviously deludes us. So does defining ourselves by what others do.

NOTICING WHAT OTHERS DO

Many years ago I took our kids to visit my beloved Nana. She, of course, fell in love with them. I can still see the warm smile on her face when she said, "You must be a good mom. You have such good children." They're good; I'm good. I softened at her words. Then I started to feel a little uneasy. If they misbehave, does that make me a bad mom? I took a breath, and checked on them out of the corner of my eye. They were doing okay, and I exhaled. I was okay too, at least for the moment.

What a precarious and costly (not to mention stupid) way to live. Having to control their behavior was even more exhausting than trying to control my own. Thinking they could define me was both scary and inaccurate, while putting such a burden on them was unfair. Another bad choice comes to light. So does another error: thinking that someone else's activity can change who I am. If we're not careful to avoid this fallacy, we'll end up (once again) with pseudoworth.

Beyond the pseudoworth arising from our "more than" or "better than" comparisons, we often make another error that leads to a false view of self: we accept someone else's thoughts without evaluating the truth of their opinion.

BELIEVING WHAT OTHERS THINK

No one else's ideas about us determine who we are. Whatever they think, whatever they say, other people can't alter our identity. Most of us don't believe this. Instead we give a lot of weight to how we look in others' eyes.

Both positive and negative inputs impact us deeply. Have you ever stumbled during a presentation, seen a smirk on a co-worker's face, and instantly felt less valuable than yesterday's trash? Can you remember a time when you glanced across the room, saw a grin in a friend's eyes, and found their welcome boosting your confidence?

Shame or praise, inclusion or exclusion, a blow or a caress – though they feel so different they're alike in an important way: each of them is a message from another person. And others may or may not be telling us the truth, particularly about who we are.

Please understand. I'm not minimizing the discomfort of a negative interaction or ignoring the pleasure that affirmation brings. I'm simply saying that no one else's response to us can alter who we are.

Pseudoworth Summarized

While our value never changes, our sense of value often fluctuates dramatically. It does so because we've opted for a self-manufactured worth, pseudoworth, that false self we substitute for the self whom God has created.

Self is not stuff, identity is not activity, and you don't determine who I am.

Pseudoworth tempts us all. We assume that what we have defines us. We assume that what we do defines us. We compare ourselves with others and assume that what they have and do defines us. We assume that what others think defines us. Just like Walter Mitty, we invent imaginary selves. Unlike Walter, the selves we imagine may cause us to flinch rather than to smile.

Pseudoworth is exhausting, yet we struggle on, trying to produce a worth we know we must have. Depression and anxiety wear our reserves transparently thin as we work to be acceptable, lovable, includable, special. We're burning out because of ignorance – we don't understand that we're already special far beyond anything we've ever longed for. There's no need for pseudoworth – God has made us like Himself. "I value you" signs are posted throughout the Bible. Only the blind ignore them.

Defined by God

Pseudoworth is a human product; real worth is defined by God. God uses Himself as a plumb line. Old-school carpenters held these weighted ropes next to a door frame to tell if the studs were upright or tilting off-center. God puts His image next to us and says we're like Him. He puts His worth next to ours, and says we're worthwhile.

Worth comes from God. Not from possessions, not from efforts, and not from others. We're not defined by what we have or by what we do; not by other people and not by self. We're made in God's image, defined by Him.

That's incredible news. And we have a problem.

DISTORTED BY ADAM

We still bear God's image, but the image has changed from a dream come true into a nightmare.

The nightmare started when Adam, joy of God's heart, ignored his Creator. One bite of fruit, quickly taken but never forgotten. It only took a moment. By one swallow Adam altered his future, and ours.

Adam's rebellion distorted in a deadly way the image God had given him. He's passed this distortion on to us; it's part of our inheritance. While God's image has continued through the generations, it no longer contains His life. Worth remains, but its expression is severely handicapped.

Death has begun.

NOTES

CHAPTER 9 – DIFFERENTIATING SELF FROM OTHERS

1. God says that *all* fall short of His glory, and that He will graciously rescue *all* who believe.

    *Romans 3:21 But now apart from the Law the righteousness of God has been manifested, being witnessed by the Law and the Prophets, 22 even the righteousness of God through faith in Jesus Christ for **all** those who believe; for there is no distinction; 23 for **all** have sinned and fall short of the glory of God, 24 being justified as a gift by His grace through the redemption which is in Christ Jesus.*

PART III
Death Begins

Part III Overview
Death Begins

When Adam rebels against God, his decision profoundly alters his identity. Though the image of God is not lost, it is damaged: Adam's living self morphs into a dead caricature of God's original design; his initial beauty suffers a deep and devastating change. Adam, the living being, is now Adam, the dying being.

Adam's death spreads to us all. Each of us starts our life physically alive but spiritually dead. We all bear the damaged image brought about by Adam's act. God will provide a way to restore that damaged image to its original aliveness, but before we can appreciate His re-creation of life, we must understand the death from which we need rescue.

The third part of this book reveals our desperate need for release from death. Chapter 10, *The Entrance of Death*, describes Adam's deadly rebellion. Chapter 11, *The Spread of Death*, connects Adam's rebellion with the spread of death throughout the world and shows how Adam's choice to disobey God affects us all.

How does Adam's death impact you?

10
The Entrance of Death

So far, life, only life, has been present in Genesis. Adam is about to add death to the picture.

His is such a small act and over so quickly. A short reach of the arm, a grasp, a taste, a swallow. With one bite of fruit, Adam alters his future, and ours. His actions seem so insignificant until you consider the heart behind it. Adam is ignoring God.

Perhaps he thinks he's doing no more than looking after himself, but make no mistake, this is rebellion. Adam chooses his own way over God's. His infidelity comes with unanticipated and deadly consequences.

Adam Changes Everything

We don't get to choose the consequences of our choices. There's no getting around it. Sin, every time and always, results in death.[1] Adam has the unenviable distinction of being the first to trigger this process.

This man's revolt flies in the face of God's command and clear warning:

> *Genesis 2:17 But from the tree of the knowledge of good and evil you shall not eat; for in the day that you eat from it you will surely die.*[2]

In this verse, God is speaking only to the man. Each "you" – and there are three of them – refers to Adam.[3] The Lord pointedly gives Adam a command: from the tree of the knowledge of good and evil you, *Adam*, shall not eat. God's warning to the man is equally direct: on the day that you, *Adam*, eat from it, you, *Adam*, the living being, will surely die. We can hear the ominous, slow notes of a string bass in the background as God's words make a shiver run up our spines.

Adam should have shivered also. Instead, he turns away from God's voice, and dismisses God's words:

> *Genesis 3:6 When the woman saw that the tree was good for food, and that it was a delight to the eyes, and that the tree was desirable to make one wise, she took from its fruit and ate, **and she gave also to her husband with her, and he ate**.*

Adam ate. His was the pivotal act – God makes that quite clear. Not only does the command and warning in Genesis 2 concern Adam's eating, but the structure of Genesis 3:6 focuses a spotlight on him – the words used in that verse emphasize Adam's action.[4] His choice brings death. He is responsible for guarding their life.

And when Adam fails they both die.⁵

You may be used to blaming Eve for bringing death into the world, and it's true that she eats first, but Adam's eating is what changes everything. As the fruit moves from his hand into his stomach, death begins in paradise.

DEATH OF SELF

When Adam swallows, they both die. But wait – they don't seem dead. If we'd been there, we would see them do all kinds of things that "living" people do: put on clothes, run around and hide, talk, blame, make love, have kids, work, eat, drink, breathe the air. I'd think they're alive; God says they're dead. Even though we can believe (though in a far-off, abstract sort of way) that God is telling us the truth, we're still left wondering. What dies?

What dies is that living, invisible, spiritual self made in God's image. *They* die, on the inside, and their death – a death of self – profoundly alters all they have and do and think and feel and choose. Their physical bodies still work, though now with aches and pains. Their minds function, although not as clearly. Their emotions flow, but often in skewed directions. Their wills can still choose, though the choices bend toward rebellion. But Adam and Eve? They are dead.

One swallow, by one man, and death makes its terrifying entrance. Even imagining Adam's experience makes me shudder. He must have had one of those awful moments that twist the pit of our stomachs, the kind we get when we realize we've done a terrible thing and can never take it back. Adam couldn't take his swallow back. He eats, chills as his own life goes cold, watches the joy leave his wife's eyes, and feels his horror spread as everything around him starts to groan.[6] When Adam eats, living spiritual beings become dead spiritual beings, and everything on earth suffers along with them.

DEAD OR ALIVE – HOW CAN YOU TELL?

Adam and Eve are dead, spiritually dead. The only reason they don't seem dead is because we're not very good at distinguishing spiritual life and death. But physical life and death? Those we can tell apart. That's helpful. Because what happens spiritually isn't all that different from what happens physically. Let me clarify with a story. It's about frogs.

Quite a few years ago our family – my husband, our children, and I – took a vacation to Hawaii. We settled into a great rental unit near the beach: no kitchen (no cooking!), a little sitting room, two bedrooms, and two baths (one with shower, one with tub).

One afternoon the kids went out exploring while my husband and I took a relaxing walk. A little later when we all arrived back at the unit we noticed how happy the kids looked. They must have had a great time wandering around. Everyone was hungry, so we left to get some dinner, ate, and arrived contentedly back at our rooms. That's when I found the frogs.

My kids know me pretty well. They're quite familiar with my strengths and weaknesses, and, of course, with my few minor phobias, like frogs. Do you know any kid that will overlook a chance to check out their mom's startle reflex? Not mine. During their afternoon jaunt they'd noticed that frogs kept getting caught in the resort's pool filter. Out of the kindness of their hearts they rescued all those frogs; they rescued them right into our tub. I walked casually into their bath (why were they following me?), flinched back from the squirming tub, and raced out the bathroom door. I headed straight for our room to get my husband. That's when I saw it: another frog, crouched motionless on our bed.

I'll leave the rest to your imagination – the story could use a different ending. What if I'd had the presence of mind (okay, the courage) to check out that frog in our bedroom and see if it were dead or alive. How would I find out?

Since I'd never touch a frog, I'd have to grab something, a broom maybe, and poke at it. If my poke does no more than scrape the frog's body across the bedclothes, then it's dead. (Yes!) But if my poke startles the frog and it jumps at me, then it's alive. I'll know it's alive because it responds to my touch. That's what living frogs do.

That's what living people do too, both physically and spiritually. Those who are physically alive are able to respond physically to physical touch; if they're dead they can't. Those who are spiritually alive are able to respond spiritually to God's touch. Dead spiritual beings can't.

Now please don't remember just this story. Remember its point: spiritually living people can respond to God. They can respond to Him in living ways – with love, with worship, with obedience, with joy. When Adam dies, he loses his ability to respond to God in living ways. He still walks the earth, but God's touch no longer excites him.

Adam is dead, spiritually dead. And his death has spread to us.

NOTES
CHAPTER 10 – THE ENTRANCE OF DEATH

1. Romans 6:23 *For the wages of sin is death, but the free gift of God is eternal life in Christ Jesus our Lord.*

2. The Hebrew phrase translated surely die literally means *"dying you shall die."* This is a very emphatic phrase. There was no way Adam could have missed God's meaning.

3. Each *you* in the Hebrew text is masculine singular and can only refer to Adam.

4. The Hebrew sentence balances on either side of a punctuation mark that acts like a literary fulcrum (something like the center of a seesaw). The fulcrum divides the sentence into two equally "weighty" parts. In Genesis 3:6, the sixteen Hebrew words which describe Eve's actions balance the five Hebrew words that describe her husband's involvement. Adam's section, because it has fewer words, carries more weight per word, thus giving each word about Adam more emphasis.

5. Romans 5:12 *...through one man sin entered into the world, and death through sin...* See also *Romans 5:15 ...by the transgression of the one the many died...* Adam's sin brought death not just to Eve, but to us all.

6. Romans 8:19-22 *...the whole creation groans and suffers...*

11
The Spread of Death

When Adam swallows, the image of God in him doesn't disappear, but it changes from vibrancy to corruption, from a living image into a dead mockery of its original living glory. The first human being to become alive is the first to become dead. He's also the first to pass his lifelessness on to the rest of us. Adam didn't cease to be a spiritual being when he chose his way over God's; he just ceased to be a *living* spiritual being.

A DEADLY HERITAGE

While Adam's death immediately spreads to his wife, it doesn't stop with her. His death transfers like a genetic catastrophe to each of his descendents. It transfers to us. From our birth – no, before that,

77

from our conception – we are physically alive but spiritually dead. We start our existence as beings unaroused by God's touch, by His words, or by His love.

Each of us bears the bitter aftertaste of Adam's mouthful of fruit. The self with which each of us enters this world is a warped shadow of the glorious self with which Adam started. We're still spiritual beings, but now we're the walking dead. Still imaged after God, but without inner life. Breathing with our lungs, but lacking God's breath.

I'm talking about everybody. Each cherished newborn has inherited more than Adam's spiritual nature – he's also inherited Adam's spiritual death. A baby may be alive to his parents, but he's dead to God. He really is. He'll reach out to mom and dad, but he won't reach out to God. He can't. Not unless God woos him towards a different kind of birth, one that entices him to stretch out his fingers to the face of his Lord.

A DIVINE SOLUTION

When set alongside Adam's story, the tragedies of the evening news pale into insignificance, for with Adam, death, disaster, and destruction got their start. We read the story of Adam's fatal choice in the third chapter of Genesis. The horror he began seems overwhelming, until we read the entire chapter. Although Genesis 3 describes Adam's tragic sin, the point of this chapter is not the tragedy but the way *out* of the tragedy. God's words emphasize not death but God's solution to death.

Shining from the center of Genesis 3 is our Lord's joyous promise of a Redeemer who can save us from death. The Rescuer, the Seed of the woman, is coming to solve our desperate need for life.[1] God planned our release form death long before Adam's sin. He planned it before an unspoiled Adam first walked through God's unspoiled garden. He designed our rescue before stars ever shone in the sky.

You can read the full story of His rescue in the New Testament. There, sprinkled piece by piece through the pages, God repeats every element of His first creation. I'll put those pieces together as we look next at God's second creation of life.

Notes

Chapter 11 – The Spread of Death

1. Genesis 3:15 contains the promise: *And I will put enmity between you and the woman, and between your seed and her seed; he shall bruise you on the head, and you shall bruise him on the heel.*

   The woman's *seed* (one of her offspring) will deal the serpent a head wound, a mortal blow. The seed is Jesus. At the very beginning of the Bible, thousands of years before Jesus is crucified, the Father promises that the Son will defeat both the serpent and death. The Father promises that Jesus, by His death on the cross, will buy for us a second chance at life.

   The importance of God's promise is emphasized several ways in Genesis chapter 3. First, by contrasting the brevity of the promise with the numerous words describing rebellion and its consequences. Second, by contrasting the promise's emotional tone of hope and joy with the surrounding tone of despair. And third, by placing the promise in a prominent position in the literary structure of this chapter.

PART IV
Life Begins Again:
A New Identity

Part IV Overview
Life Begins Again: A New Identity

When we accept Jesus, God recreates in us the inner life and
wholeness that Adam lost when he sinned. Adam didn't lose
his worth, but he did lose his aliveness. His identity shifted.
God's second creation, a birth from above reverses that deadly
shift. We become no longer dead but alive, no longer corrupt
but new and clean, no longer fragmented but whole in Him.
We receive a new living self.

The New Testament account of this second creation sounds
uncannily similar to the original Genesis event: living spiritual
beings reflect God's image, God blows into earthen vessels,
the Spirit hovers near at the birth of new life, new creations
spring into being, and selves become complete. The parallels
are unmistakable. God does with us what He originally did
with Adam – and we don't believe it. God gives all Christians
a gloriously alive inner being, yet most of us believe we're still
inwardly appalling.

The fourth part of this book details the changes occurring at
this birth from above. Chapters 12-15 describe the new self
given at salvation. Chapter 16 challenges Christians' tenacious
doubt that they have a new identity.

How would you describe who you are?

12
Spiritual Beings, Made in God's Image

Each person on earth is a spiritual being. Whether or not we have a relationship with God, each of us resembles Him. We all bear His image and the worth which that image conveys. You may not think of yourself as a spiritual being. Perhaps you need to rethink your position.

SPIRITUAL BEINGS

By now you should be able to mumble "spirit-wind-breath" in your sleep. You should know by heart that the image of our spirit-like Creator continues – from God to Adam and on to everybody else who shuffles around this planet. Christian or not, spiritually alive or spiritually dead, everyone who's asked who they are is entirely correct when they say, "I resemble God. I'm a spiritual being." Spiritual beings are interesting creatures. They're not only invisible; they're eternal.

Do you realize that you're going to last forever? The thought can exhilarate or terrify you, depending on whether or not you're connected to God. "*Ashes to ashes and dust to dust*" is true, but only about our bodies. While the earth-like part of us, for all practical purposes, vanishes into oblivion, we don't. We (the breath-like "we" inside) go on unendingly – that's the exhilarating or terrifying part. The cessation of a body doesn't mean the cessation of a self. Physical death doesn't bring self to an end, because spiritual beings don't disappear; they (living or dead) last for all eternity.

But whatever their condition, dead or alive, everybody at the core has a spiritual nature. Who are we? We're spiritual beings. And that's only the beginning of what God has to tell us.

MADE IN GOD'S IMAGE

Image, likeness, likeness, image. You can mumble that too – the Old Testament creation story is easily recalled. But did you know that the New Testament tells the same story? Even the vocabulary is familiar. Millennia after Adam, God's image and likeness are still topics of Biblical conversation:

> *1 Corinthians 11:7 For a man... is the **image** and glory **of God**[1]*
>
> *James 3:9 With [the tongue] we bless our Lord and Father; and with it we curse men, who have been made in the **likeness of God**[2]*

In these two passages God has used Genesis language[3] to connect Adam's creation with our own. Since the beginning of time everyone without exception resembles God.

I personally would have thought that our resemblance to God was
lost when Adam died. I know it wasn't, but I find myself puzzled.
Though I believe it, I don't quite understand it. Nonetheless, God's
image still is identifiable, even after being warped by death. I'm
reminded of the story about stretching out that legendary dollar
bill. If we pulled each end just right perhaps George would flash
us a macabre sort of grin. The stretching would, of course, warp
George's image, but we still could recognize him (even if we cringed
at his dental work).

We certainly cringe at times when we look at each other. Like a
stretched out George, everyone resembles God, but in a distorted
and twisted sort of way. Many people produce a pretty good show
of acting alive, but it's not real – a lot of God's image-bearers
remain dead. Dead, that is, until the Father-Son-Spirit God blows
life into the image-bearers who accept His call. But whether
spiritually dead or spiritually alive, each person still calls God to
mind. Adam and your eccentric Uncle Fred and you and I. We all
bear the image and likeness of God.

Being God's image-bearer has very practical implications. Many of
you picked up this book because you were unsure about your
identity. You dared to hope that something in here
would convince you that you have at least a modest
amount of value. The truth is sweet and the reality is
better than your wildest hopes. Let this sink in: you
resemble God. The One who defines value doesn't

We resemble God.
His worth is the
foundation for
our worth

hoard His value, but passes it on to us. What a fine, sweet, and firm
foundation for self-worth.

But self-worth is only part of the picture. What about other people?

Judging others

Don't start at this point to become enamored with yourself;
you don't get to claim your own significance while you deny
significance to others. They have value too. Take your neighbor –
the one who never mows his lawn and lets his trash slop over onto
your driveway. That neighbor. The one made in the image of God.
Or what about the stranger this morning who cut in front of you
to grab the last parking space? "Stupid idiot," you mutter to the
steering wheel. That idiot. The one made in the image of God.
What about him?

The truth is unsettling: each time we put someone down (whether
we think it or spew it from our mouth) we assume that one of
God's image-bearers is worthless. Perhaps we don't consciously
think *worthless*, but that word does reflect the attitude of our hearts.
Disgust at a messy neighbor ignores his likeness to God. So does
disdain for a pushy driver. Even as we respond to their actions, we
mustn't forget to notice *them*, the person behind the action. We
mustn't fail to notice that they resemble God.

I know this – that everyone resembles God – but sometimes I
forget. A few moments ago, I was admiring a truly fine sentence
I'd just written (something about everyone bearing the image of
God) when the phone rang. Another inane phone solicitor was
calling to interrupt what they assumed was my dinner hour. I was
courteous (though appropriately firm) on the phone, hung up the
receiver, and came back to my computer. But instead of writing,
I started savoring several pointed and clever remarks I could have
made to the caller on the other end of the line. I couldn't believe it
–my caustic thoughts totally contradicted what I'd written. I had
to rethink my attitude. *Could phone solicitors also be made in the
image of God?*

As awful as it is that we do this with each other, something worse is going on – the way we treat people parallels how we treat God.[4]

Judging God

Every time we sneer at a person (including ourselves) we're also sneering at the One who made that person. Imagine a group of us standing in a museum ridiculing a sculpture when we suddenly notice the artist hovering next to his creation. Did he hear us? If he did, we'd likely feel uneasy, perhaps ashamed.

Sculpted in stone or formed by God, creations reveal their Creator, and ridiculing someone's creation amounts to ridiculing them. Belittling people is belittling God. Laughing at people is laughing at God. Judging people is judging God. Our attitude to any creation reveals our attitude to its creator. How do you treat people? That's how you're treating God.

Making that connection is uncomfortable because none of us can wiggle out of it; we've all participated in this spectator sport. But don't pull back from your discomfort. You won't change your behavior unless you stay aware that a put down to a human being, any human being, whether in words, deeds, or thoughts, is a put down to God. Our similarity to Him is that pronounced. As you know, each of us calls Him to mind.

REMEMBERING THE TRUTH

What if we never forgot that our spouse, or sibling, or child bears God's image? What if we stopped criticizing and condemning and putting them down? Wouldn't that change our family life! I'm not talking about stuffing issues, and I don't mean ignoring differences, but I do mean recognizing and honoring each person – the person inside – regardless of their current behavior. Even as we respond to what they're doing, we never are to respond in a way that demeans their dignity. We must remember the presence of God's image in each person we meet.

We also must remember the presence of God's image in ourselves. Do you ever demean your own dignity? Can you honestly look at your choices or emotions or actions without condemning who you are? Do you ever forget that you resemble God?

Wouldn't it be something if we kept in mind that everyone bears God's image? How our relationships would change if we remembered that all of us, each of us, like God, have great worth built into us. But we forget. We forget that everyone – your enemy, your friend, yourself – no matter what they do, even when they're acting like a jerk, should be treated with the dignity due an image-bearer of God. As I said before, everyone has the family nose.

Our universal resemblance to God adds to the description of who we are: we are *spiritual beings created by God in His likeness and image.*

This likeness to God is wonderful, but incomplete – a crucial element is still missing. Are people spiritual? Yes. Image-bearers? Yes. But alive? Not necessarily. A transformation is needed, and, as you might expect, it comes through God's breath.

NOTES

CHAPTER 12 – SPIRITUAL BEINGS, MADE IN GOD'S IMAGE

1. *Image* translates the Greek word *eikon*, which means image or likeness. *Eikon* is the counterpart of the Hebrew word *tselem*, translated as *image* in Genesis 1:26-27.

2. *Likeness* translates the Greek word *homoiosis*, which means likeness or resemblance. *Homoiosis* is the counterpart of the Hebrew word *damut*, translated as *likeness* in Genesis 1:26.

3. *Genesis 1:26-27.*

4. *Matthew 25:34-45.*
   (Note particularly verses 40 and 45):
   40 And the King will answer and say to them, "Truly I say to you, to the extent that you did it to one of these brothers of Mine, even the least of them, you did it to Me." ... 45 Then He will answer them, saying, "Truly I say to you, to the extent that you did not do it to one of the least of these, you did not do it to Me."

13
Made Alive by God's Breath

Everyone qualifies as spiritual. Everyone qualifies as an image-bearer. But not everyone qualifies as alive, at least not as spiritually alive. Spiritual life requires God's breath.

God's breath alters our self. His alterations to self don't change our worth; they simply make us able to respond to Him.

BIRTH BY BREATH

You see it first in Adam's creation. Breath. Breath. Breath. Breath. Breath. Life. Life. Breath to life. What God does with Adam, He now offers us. Thousands of years after God breathes into Adam, the Son imitates His Father. Look at the astonishing thing Jesus does with His disciples:

*John 20:22 And when He [Jesus] had said this, He **breathed** on them and said to them "Receive the Holy **Spirit**."*

This is one of those odd verses you've probably ignored because it didn't make sense. Think again. Jesus has just revisited Genesis 2:7.

Breath to life. The words remind us of Adam's creation, and so they should. Adam becomes a living being when *God* blows the Spirit into him. The disciples of Jesus become living beings when *Jesus* blows the Spirit into them. If you've assumed the Holy Spirit arrives a bit later, after Jesus ascends into heaven,[1] Jesus' act may startle you. But even more startling than His "premature" gift of the Holy Spirit is the claim Jesus makes by His act.

Take a minute to consider what Jesus is doing. While His act does foreshadow the coming of the Holy Spirit, that's only part of the event. This is a parable in action. When Jesus breathes on His disciples He demonstrates, unmistakably, that He is God.

Let that sink in. Jesus deliberately repeats God's act in Genesis. By replicating God's action – and with the same results – Jesus claims deity. Everyone present would have known exactly what He meant.

Breath to life. Jesus breathes the Holy Spirit towards the disciples, and they breathe in. He offers us the same experience: God the Son breathes the Holy Spirit towards us; we can breathe in too.

Who, then, are we? If we've breathed in God's life, we are spiritual beings, created by God in His likeness and image, transformed by God's breath. Transformed spiritually, altered on the inside, changed from dead to alive.

FROM DEATH TO LIFE

As you know (remember the frogs), death, physical or spiritual, has a downside. Little babies stir as their mom strokes their cheek and, with trembling lips, turn to her nourishment. They don't have the same responsiveness to God. Deadened spiritual nerve endings don't permit them to sense His presence. They, and we, start our earth-time insensitive to God's touch. God solves that deficit through a spiritual transformation; He changes dead selves into living ones. Paul tells us so in Ephesians:

> *Ephesians 2:4 But God, being rich in mercy, because of His great love with which He loved us, 5 even when we were **dead** in our transgressions, made us **alive** together with Christ (by grace you have been saved)...*

Paul knows about God's death-to-life transformation first hand. When Jesus meets him on the road to Damascus,[2] Paul is a dead man walking. The story doesn't mention these details, but we know what happens. Jesus breathes out, Paul breathes in, and is shaken to the core with the first real life he's ever smelled.

Frankly, Paul doesn't deserve the break; his resume features an jolting bullet point: tormenter of Christians. But as Paul heads to another malicious confrontation, Jesus confronts him – and gives him life. Life! That's not fair. Paul doesn't qualify for such a gift. But that's the point. Gifts are an act of grace; gifts aren't earned, but given freely.

Paul knows he doesn't deserve God's gift. That's why he describes God as he does – rich in mercy, loving, gracious, a God who gives what we need, not what we deserve. Paul is bursting to tell us his amazing discovery: the God of the universe gives lavish, undeserved gifts.

Do you see God as a lavish gift giver? Your life will change, and change remarkably, once you believe that He delights to offer us outlandish and undeserved gifts. Not boringly proper gifts, like a three-pack of white socks for Christmas, but real gifts, like turning your inner death and emptiness into life and joy.

GOD IN LABOR

When Paul writes the Ephesians about death and life he doesn't mean funerals and birth announcements. The life Paul describes goes way beyond the physical. Physical birth won't get us the kind of life we need. For real life, spiritual life – the kind of life that lasts forever – we must be born from above. For our first birth our moms labor, but the second time it's all the work of God.

> *Ephesians 2:10 For we are **His** workmanship, created in Christ Jesus...*

This is important enough to take slowly. We are His workmanship. His workmanship – not our own workmanship. No wiggle room exists here, no suggestion that we partner with God to produce life. God creates life all by Himself. Without our help. As with Adam, our contribution is zero.

If God is telling us the truth (and I'm deeply sure He is), then our own efforts to get life are, bluntly said, useless. Do we think we can't stand one more bout of internal numbness or manage to live through another season of pervasive dreariness and pressure? When we exhaust ourselves trying to connect with some facsimile of aliveness bubbling up within us, do our efforts help? No. We can't pull it off. Well, perhaps we'll taste a short-term fix, but nothing that lasts. When it comes to getting life we are quite helpless.

I try to avoid feeling helpless, primarily because I hate feeling vulnerable. Doing something, anything, feels much safer than waiting and praying and trusting God to act, especially if we're after something essential, like life. It seems so much easier to ignore our limitations and start looking for what we can achieve: life-substitutes.

Most of our life-substitutes seem good at the moment. A glass more of Merlot might help (well, maybe not Merlot). Perhaps some other chemical will ease our emptiness. If not, there's always sex, eating, showing-off, or taking crazy risks (nothing like that adrenaline rush). Some of our substitutes are okay in themselves, and some aren't, but none of them give more than a transient rush. Substitutes don't yield real life. They're all temporary fixes.

Creating real life, life that lasts, is the work of God. The stories in the Bible catch Him in the act: God's Breath invades Adam;[3] the Spirit invades Mary;[4] a mighty rushing Wind invades the disciples.[5] Each event is a birth from above,[6] and in each God brings real life, the kind that won't fade away.

BIRTH BY SPIRIT

Jesus gives us the facts in His conversation with Nicodemus.

> *John 3:3 Jesus answered and said to [Nicodemus], "Truly, truly, I say to you, unless one is born again, he cannot see the kingdom of God." 4 Nicodemus said to Him, "How can a man be born when he is old? He cannot enter a second time into his mother's womb and be born, can he?" 5 Jesus answered, "Truly, truly, I say to you, unless one is **born of water and the Spirit** he cannot enter into the kingdom of God. 6 That which is **born of the flesh** is flesh, and that which is **born of the Spirit** is **Spirit**. 7 Do not be amazed that I said to you, 'You must be born again.'"*

When Jesus tells Nicodemus that he must be born again (literally, "born from above") to enter into the kingdom of heaven, Nicodemus gets confused. He hears the word *born*, focuses on the

literal scenario, and pointedly reminds Jesus that His idea is, to say
the least, unworkable. Jesus clarifies: "No. No. I don't mean re-birth
from your mother; I'm talking about birth from the Spirit. You
need *spiritual* life."

Don't let Jesus' unfamiliar language confuse you. Born of water and
born of the flesh both refer to a physical birth, which, as expected,
produces a physical baby. But born of the Spirit? That starts a
spiritual life.

Then and now, the Spirit continues to invade the death within us
and produce living children of God – with Mary, with Nicodemus,
and with us.

BIRTH BY WIND

In Acts, Luke connects this birth-giving Spirit with the wind:

> *Acts 2:2 And suddenly there came from heaven a noise like a*
> *violent rushing **wind**, and it filled the whole house where they*
> *were sitting. 3 And there appeared to them tongues as of fire*
> *distributing themselves, and then rested on each one of them.*
> *4 And they were all filled with the Holy **Spirit**...*

Birth by breath for Adam. Birth by breath for the disciples. Birth
by Spirit for Mary and Nicodemus. Birth by wind in the upper
room. Are you getting the connection? I hope so. Who brings us
to life? The spirit-like, wind-like, breath-like God. And what kind
of life is given? Spirit-like, wind-like breath-like life. In this deep
and intimate way we take after our heavenly parent. Don't treat our
resemblance to God as a cold impersonal fact. Please don't. Because
our likeness to Him is personally and profoundly true.

At this point how do we describe God's birth-children? If we've breathed in God's life, we are spiritual beings, created by God in His likeness and image, *made alive by God's breath*.

And what else?

NOTES

CHAPTER 13 – MADE ALIVE BY GOD'S BREATH

1. *Acts 1:1-9* and *2:1-4.*

2. *Acts 9:1-17.*

3. *Genesis 2:7.*

4. *Matthew 1:20.* The Holy Spirit enters Mary's body and a living baby begins within her.

5. *Acts 2:1-4.*

6. God describes a woman's act, giving birth, to illustrate for us the reality of His birthing us spiritually. In the Bible God frequently assigns to Himself either male or female roles, including father and mother, to illustrate His character. Remember, though, that God is neither male nor female – God is Spirit. (Male and female are human categories.)

14

New Creations, in Earthen Houses

The Old Testament-New Testament parallels get even stronger. Like Adam, our newly created selves inhabit earth-like bodies. The echo of the first creation continues.

New Creations

Millennia after the first event, a new creation takes place, one that allows deep intimacy with Jesus Christ. People created anew in Him experience such a dramatic shift that they identify themselves with a new name, His name. They call themselves Christians.

Paul identifies Christians another way; he calls them new creatures.

> *2 Corinthians 5:17 Therefore if anyone is in Christ, he is a **new creature**; the old things passed away; behold, **new** things have come.*

Paul's word *creature* matches the word *create* used in Genesis.[1] His word *new*, however, holds a surprise. That word points to things that never before existed, not just new in time, but new in essence. When Paul says new he's talking about something startlingly unique.

Anyone and everyone who's breathed in Christ has been changed into someone distinctly new. Unfamiliar. Foreign to past experience. Different enough from the ordinary to penetrate someone's awareness and cause them to step back (or perhaps forward) and wonder, *What is that?*

I wondered the same thing when we moved to the West Coast. A neighbor a few houses down kept inviting me over for tea. I knew she was a Christian, but she never actually talked to me about her faith. If she had I would've walked out of her house. This was my B.C. (before Christ) period, and I was less than interested to hear anything about Jesus. So she made me tea and fed me cookies, chatted with me about myself, and all the while was really patient with her toddler twins. Patient and kind and peaceful; none of these qualified as my strong suit.

While we talked, I watched. Something different was right there in front of me, and that something pulled at me. I wanted what she had. I wanted it badly. Though I couldn't exactly see it, I could sense it, almost inhale it. It turned out to be Jesus. He'd made her new and then had me smell His fragrance wafting from her character.[2] Later on, in large part because of her, I asked for His newness for myself.

Newness, invisible but perceivable, expands this description of who we are. If we've breathed in God's life, we are living spiritual beings, created by God in His likeness and image, transformed by God's breath, made into *new creations* – new selves.

EARTHEN HOUSES

Each new self moves into a used house, the same house the old self called home. In Genesis 2 God molds *earth* into a manly form. Now, in 2 Corinthians, Paul calls our bodies *earthen* vessels.

> *2 Corinthians 4:7 But we have this **treasure in earthen vessels**, so that the surpassing greatness of the power will be of God and not from ourselves;*

As with Adam, so with us. The first creation/second creation parallels continue.

When Paul says vessels he isn't talking about jars of olive oil, he's talking about human bodies, and when he says treasure he doesn't mean a stash of coins, he means the Holy Spirit. While the treasure is spiritual, our bodies are made from ordinary stuff, the same elements we find in dirt. Bodies are simply mud-like containers, nothing special – except that they contain God's breath. Does this sound familiar? It should.

> *Adam was Earth + Breath I. Believers are Earth + Breath II.*

Because God blows into us the same treasure He blew into Adam.

Now who are we? If we've breathed in God's life, we are living spiritual beings, created by God in His likeness and image, transformed by God's breath, *new creations dwelling in earthly bodies.*

The description is almost finished. What else characterizes us? Completeness.

Notes

Chapter 14 – New Creations, in Earthen Houses

1. The Greek word for creation, *ktisis*, translates as either *creature* or *creation*. In 2 Corinthians 5:17, Paul says that anyone in Christ is a new *ktisis* – a new *creature*, a new *creation*. The parallel verb, to create, *ktizo*, also appears in the Bible, both in the New Testament and in the Greek translation of the Hebrew Old Testament.

   Ktizo translates the Hebrew word for create, *barah*. The Hebrew *barah* and its Greek counterpart *ktizo* are the words used in Genesis 1:1 and 1:27 to describe God's original creation. These words appear again in Psalm 51:10 when David pleas for God to create in him a clean heart. Both words refer to the powerful and unique work of God to create the world, to create David's clean heart, and to create our clean, new selves.

2. *2 Corinthians 2:15 For we are a fragrance of Christ to God among those who are being saved and among those who are perishing; 16 to the one an aroma from death to death, to the other an aroma from life to life....*

15
Complete

God says that He has made us complete. Check out His words for yourself:

Colossians 2:10 and in Him you **have been made complete**...

Notice the timing of God's words: *have been*. Making us complete is a past act, something already accomplished which will continue to affect our current lives.

You may find yourself balking at what God has said. The whole idea of being complete seems so outlandish that most of us skip quickly past the concept and scan ahead for something that will make more sense. That's a mistake. If you don't stop to savor the word *complete*, you'll miss its startling implications.

Think for a moment about sponges. Have you ever seen those hard little yellow sponges that come compressed ten to a package? I get a charge out of dropping them one at the time into a bowl of hot water and watching them morph into soft big yellow sponges that I can lift dripping out of the bowl. You can even get tiny sponge dinosaurs that'll do the same thing; they're the best. When you lift an engorged Tyrannosaurus Rex out of the water, the excess liquid just drips down its stubby legs and off the end of its tail. (Yes, I am easily amused.) But that's how sponges work. Each one, put into liquid, absorbs all it can hold, and then some, until it fills and overflows.

Sponges are the perfect analogy. They function like we're made to function. Sponges, when put into regular water, soak it up; we, when put into living water (into God[1]) soak Him up. We're immersed into God to absorb all of Him we can hold – and then some – until, from deep within us, His presence overflows.[2] This is where the idea of complete comes in. Paul uses a word for complete that means filled to overflowing.[3]

When Paul says complete he's assuring us of the presence in ourselves of a kind of water – spiritual living water – so plentiful that it will spill over our edges and pour out into the world. New selves are completely – beyond completely – filled with Him. There are no empty, or ugly, spaces in self.

God's Truth ... Our Experience

God says we're complete. Now for our experience. Most of us (with responses ranging from occasional bouts of uneasiness to episodes of bone-chilling dismay) are sure that we, at our core, are missing something essential.

God may consider us complete, but we have a lot of trouble believing Him. With our shortcomings so glaringly apparent to us, how could we be complete? Our thought life definitely isn't all it could be, our emotions often run amuck, and it's embarrassingly obvious that our behavior could greatly improve. God says "complete"? We think not. We don't see much that *looks* complete.

Our doubts linger like moldy leftovers from our pre-Jesus years: before we received His life something really was missing. But no longer. If we've breathed in Christ, incompleteness is, quite literally, past tense.

Do you still think you're incomplete? In a limited sense, you're right – you are incomplete, but only in what you do. All of us could use significant changes in our thoughts, emotions, and behavior. But as for who we *are* – that's been finished. Nothing needs to be added to our identity, either to make us worthwhile or to enable us to express God's character. Even with all the needed improvement, there's no need for "*self*-improvement," not any more. God completes self-improvement the moment He enters us. He, in us, makes us permanently and indisputably complete.

WHO ARE WE?

If we've breathed in God's life, we are living spiritual beings, created by God in His likeness and image, transformed by God's breath, dwelling in earthen vessels, and made into new creations who are *complete in Him.*

This is who God says we are. But, though His description of us is accurate, we aren't quite comfortable with His conclusions. We harbor some doubts.

NOTES

CHAPTER 15 – COMPLETE

1. While God does blow Himself into us, He also immerses us in Himself. Like interlaced fingers, He is in us and we are in Him. (See Colossians 3:3 ...our lives are hidden with Christ in God. See also John 14:20 where Jesus says His disciples are in Him and He is in them, and Jeremiah 17:13 where God is called living water.)

2. *John 7:38 He who believes in Me [Jesus]...from his innermost being shall flow streams of living water. 39 But this He spoke of the Spirit..*

3. The word complete, from the Greek *pleroo*, means made full, fully supplied, complete. In Colossians 2:10, the word occurs in the Greek perfect tense. This tense refers to an action completed in the past yet with continuing effects into the present. (Think about this. How would believing that you are already complete change your everyday life?)

16
And Doubtful

You may find it difficult to agree with God that He has transformed us in such remarkable ways. You're not alone. Most Christians don't understand the suddenness or permanence of the inner changes God produces.

WHAT GOD SAYS

Contrary to widely-spread Christian dogma, Jesus breathes each new creation into being suddenly, instantly. True, behavior changes gradually, but self changes abruptly. The moment we take our first spiritual breath old selves become new, dead selves become alive, and incomplete selves become complete.

> *Behavior changes gradually.*
> *Self changes abruptly.*

The good news gets better: unlike Adam, our life can't be lost. Are you alive in Christ? Have you accepted His gift of Himself? Then you can be confident that He will never isolate you from His life-giving presence. Once invited in, Jesus not only refuses to leave, but also will never allow you to leave Him. He tells you so Himself:

> *Hebrews 13:5 ...for He Himself has said,* **"I will never desert you, nor will I ever forsake you."**

Literally translated His promise is both stronger and clearer. Jesus speaks to calm our hearts*: never, never will I let go of you* [so we can't leave Him], and *never, never, never will I go away from you* [He won't leave us]. Case closed.

What We See

Such good news. It sounds too good to be true. The good news doesn't look very true either. Glance around at other Christians. Don't you doubt (at least occasionally) that God has done anything new with them? Look at your own thoughts and feelings for a more pronounced jolt – it probably looks like He hasn't changed you much either. God's good news apparently has had little effect.

With persistence, God contradicts our pessimism. He tells us He's made us new. He says we're different, but we keep seeing more of the same. How can we believe that God knows the facts when His version sounds more like a fairy tale? Is a new self only a pipe dream? Could God's good news, at least for our time on earth, be no more than a delusion?

What We Don't See

God certainly seems delusional. He says He's given us a new self, we can't see it, and conclude that God has done nothing. At least not with us. The lack of visible evidence is compelling, often more convincing than the words of an invisible God who contradicts our eyes.

Do you delight in who you are? I don't mean some sort of abstract feeling that you're probably okay. I mean joy. Most of us never come close to joy, particularly about ourselves. Instead of delighting in our new identity, we're blind to its presence and wary to trust that newness and glory permeate the depths of our being. God has given us a new self; we can't see it, and the lack of visual evidence convinces most of us that God, though He may change others, has withheld such change from us. We try to trust His Word, yet we struggle when we can't see the reality He describes.

The problem is not with reality and not with God. It's with us. When we try to see spiritual realities – like new selves – with physical eyes, we get at best only shadows of what's there. Invisible selves are obscured from physical eyes.

To know our new identity we need new eyes, spiritual eyes that are able to perceive God's truth. To get these eyes we need a uniquely skilled eye doctor, both to give us our new eyes and to teach us how to use them.

PART V
Blindness to Sight

PART V OVERVIEW
BLINDNESS TO SIGHT

Christians have a new self. That's a fact. But that fact doesn't ensure that we'll *believe* we've been changed and doesn't guarantee that we'll *differentiate* who we now are from who we were.

The fifth part of this book sorts out our unbelief and confusion. Chapter 17, *Blind Men Walking*, points out our trouble seeing reality. Chapter 18, *Pirates, Mirrors, and Glory*, tells how we can perceive what can't be directly seen. Chapter 19, *Expectations and Exhaustion*, shows how our efforts to "act new" drain us of energy. Chapter 20, *Double Vision, Single Self,* exposes the typical (and erroneous) Christian confusion of flesh with self. Chapter 21, *Not Self but Sin*, clearly differentiates between self and that ungodly flesh-sin-death trio. Chapter 22, *Double World, Single Focus,* helps us experience the new self that God has already produced.

Do you delight in who you are?
Do you think God delights in who you are?

17
Blind Men Walking

We truly are blind, and because of our handicap are hesitant to trust that we, like the freshly created Adam, are unblemished selves.

BLIND TO THE LANDSCAPE

Some 20 years later I can still see the blind student tapping his way towards class with his long, red-tipped cane. My son and I stared in unison at his slow but steady progress. Sensing a "teachable moment" (I was probably trying to instill compassion or something), I commented how hard it must be to get around when you're blind. Just like that my son became my teacher: "It's a lot better than being blind and staying home." He was right.

The blind men in the Gospel stories didn't stay home, and I don't think they had those special canes or their own Seeing Eye dogs. From the stories, at least half of them didn't even have anybody holding on to their elbow. I can picture them searching out Jesus' voice, tripping over rocks, scraping their toes in their eagerness to reach His healing touch. If you're blind, not to the landscape, but to who you are, you'd better find the same doctor they used – the ophthalmologist from above.

The blind men seeking Jesus were desperate to see. How about you? Wouldn't it be something to have vision so perfect that you'd laugh with delight (or perhaps cry with relief) as your unblemished self comes into focus. Do you want that kind of vision? You might consider asking Jesus to touch your eyes before you read on.

BLIND TO SELF

We routinely rely on visible evidence – that's clear from the way we keep scanning what we experience to see if God is telling us the truth. We look, repeatedly and anxiously, but never can catch a glimpse of that new self God says He's created. We introspect like crazy, searching for evidence of a new self, and end up seriously disappointed.

I'm not saying we don't get clues that we're new creations. Of course we do. A new self, invisible as it is, inevitably improves the things we can perceive: our behavior, our thoughts and emotions. But these noticeable changes are only evidence of a new self, not the actual new self. It's like seeing those want ads blowing down the street. You know they aren't the wind, but they do give you evidence of its presence.

The clues that God has produced internal change are clear, but they aren't consistent, and that's the problem. Side-by-side with signs of glory we perceive signs of something terribly wrong. In the middle of a friendly conversation with a neighbor, we hear ourselves make a rude comment. We're encouraged by our growing patience with our kids – until the second glass of milk spills and we explode. We enjoy cooking dinner for some friends, and then sneak the best piece of meat onto our own plate before we come to the table.

Signs of selfishness and unkindness keep challenging the signs of glory. These mixed signals leave us confused about whether we're new – or not. Visible contradictions fly in the face of God's assurance of our new identity and leave most Christians persuaded that they're flawed to the core.

CHECKING OURSELVES OUT

Most of us struggle to validate our worth by trying to bring self into view. We spend part of our time trying to see whether we are, at a minimum "okay," and spend some more of our time checking to see if we're better than the other people milling around. Believers take it a step further. We're convinced that it's actually possible (with sufficient effort) to see the new creation we've become.

All such efforts are futile. None of us succeeds in seeing self. In part, our failure occurs because we're imaged after an invisible God, but that's not the whole story.

We also can't see self because we're the ones who are doing the looking. Read on and I'll explain.

18

Pirates, Mirrors, and Glory

Picture a pirate with the requisite patch over one eye stranded on a desert island, a palm tree his only companion. Sand blows into his working eye and stings like crazy. His tears finally wash out the sand, but his eye keeps stinging, and he wonders if it's scratched. Perhaps he could pluck the eye out and turn it around so he can look at it. No, even if he could ignore the pain, that wouldn't work; his eye has moved, and all he'll see is a newly empty eye socket.

An eye can see almost everything, except itself. Eyes can't see themselves. Our pirate needs a mirror. So do we.

We need a mirror because "I's" work just like eyes. If "I" try to see "me" I'm still the one doing the looking. I suppose I could suddenly

121

whip around to try and catch a glimpse of myself, but I'd always be too late because I've moved. I've tried this trick (in jest of course) and every time I end up looking at the wall instead of at myself; I never have managed to see "me." An "I" can see almost anything – except itself. Like the pirate, I need something, actually Someone, outside of myself to tell me what I'm like. I need a mirror, just like the one Paul describes to the Corinthians:

> *2 Corinthians 3:18 But we all, with unveiled face, beholding as in a mirror the glory of the Lord, are being transformed into the same image from glory to glory, just as from the Lord, the Spirit.*

This verse is packed with information crucial to learning who we are. I'm going to unfold it carefully, phrase by phrase.

Phrase 1: with unveiled face, beholding...glory

Our faces are unveiled. Visible rather than hidden. We're being contrasted with Moses who decided to hide God's glory behind a veil.

You may recall the story. When Moses comes down from his mountain meeting with God, the skin of his face shines with God's glory. But like a great tan, this external glory doesn't last. Skin-deep glory fades.

It's different with us. Glory is carved into our very selves. That kind of glory never disappears, but stays vividly present in all its intensity and beauty. Self-deep glory never fades.

You'd think this would be great good news. But when I tell people about their unfading glory they usually turn wistful. I can almost hear them thinking: *If only that were true.*

Our fear that inner glory can fade, or even be lost, paralyzes our spontaneity. We hide. We veil our unfading glory and present a phony substitute persona to any observers; our hypocrisy masks our inner beauty.

If only that were true. If only glory never faded. Well it is true; new-creation glory doesn't fade. If Jesus has made us alive, we don't have to hide and don't have to fake it. God tells us so in His Word. When we look in the Bible – God's mirror – we'll see unveiled, unashamed, unfadingly shining beings. For believers, glory is an accomplished fact. We ought to assume its presence.

We ought to, but most of us don't.

When I meet with someone who's not so sure about inner glory, I sometimes try to talk them out of something they are sure of. Like having eyebrows.

Do you have eyebrows? ... Yes.

You're sure? ... Yes, I'm sure.

Two of them? ... Of course.

Because I only see one, on the right ...

If I kept going, at some point they'd think I'm either crazy or blind. But they would never doubt the existence of their two eyebrows. Never. No one has ever rushed to paste a patch above their left eye to hide their missing eyebrow. Nobody has patted their forehead, or asked for a mirror to check if their eyebrow is there, or pulled out an eyebrow pencil to quickly draw in the missing hairs. People are quite sure their eyebrow is there. So sure that I can't shake their confidence in its presence – even though they can't see it.

Not so with glory. It's easy to convince someone that their identity lacks glory; it's not even a challenge. What a travesty: inner glory is more solid, and much more necessary than left eyebrows. We can't live without inner glory. We need it, and we desperately need to be sure of its presence – so sure that no one can talk us out of it.

Phrase 2: beholding as in a mirror

"Mirror, mirror on the wall, who's the fairest of them all?" As the evil stepmother peered intently, she didn't see herself; she saw Snow White. That's not your typical experience.

When you look in a mirror, do you expect to see someone else's eyes staring out at you? Generally not. People who are convinced that they're evil at the core sometimes expect to see a hideous inner being looking them in the eye, but most people look in a mirror and expect to see their own face (whether least fair, fair, or fairest).

While physical mirrors show us a physical image, God's mirror is different. His mirror shows us a spiritual image: that self we can't directly see. Given our angst about our worth, it's more than a little frightening to think that our true identity might actually appear before our eyes. But don't be spooked. God's mirror doesn't show scary things like wicked stepmothers. Of course you're not going to see Snow White either, but you can look without flinching, because you're also not going to see a fiend.

Phrase 3: the glory of the Lord

When Paul talks about seeing "the glory of the Lord" in a mirror, you might think at first that he's talking about seeing God's glory. Most people think that way. Of course if Paul is telling us that this mirror gives us a glimpse of God, then when we look in it we would see something glorious – but it wouldn't be us, it would be Him.

Now I'm not saying that God isn't glorious; I'm just saying that's not what Paul is referring to in this verse. Paul isn't talking about seeing a glorious God, he's talking about seeing a glorious "me." I believe this for grammatical, logical, and relational reasons. Together I find the reasons pretty convincing.

We'll deal with the grammar first. The phrase "the glory of the Lord" can refer to God's glory. That is the party line. But there's another possible translation – an equally correct, though less popular, option – and it fits far better with what Paul is trying to say. Paul's words can also mean "the glory *from* the Lord."[1] Now that's a whole different message.

If Paul means "from the Lord" (and I'm convinced that's Paul's intent), then he is letting us know that God gives His glory away. Not only is God glorious, but He offers His glory to us. This is better than Christmas when we were three!

That's the grammatical argument, but now think about God's gift logically. Glory given to us makes sense. Paul is talking about mirrors, not about portraits. When you look at a portrait you don't necessarily see yourself, you see whomever the artist painted. But mirrors are different; mirrors reflect back the one looking in them, not someone else. When we look in God's mirror we don't see His glory shining out at us, we see our own. Our glory, a Spirit-like gift transferred to us the moment we become alive in Him.

That's the logical argument. Now think about God's gift relationally. You know how much fun it is to watch someone open a gift, made or bought doesn't matter, as long as the recipient knows it's just for them. For years our family has opened Christmas presents one gift at a time, one person at a time. I sometimes drove the kids crazy with my quirk, but I persisted. I wanted them to learn to pay attention to the interaction, to anticipate and experience the pleasure they could bring to another. And so they did. Both kids learned to anticipate and enjoy another's response to their gift. They learned to notice "somebody besides me."

God also enjoys giving. He enjoys watching as He gives us His gift of glory. He delights (with such intensity!) each time He restores shine to a tarnished image-bearer and watches not only a face but an inner self light up. God loves to give glory.

Phrase 4: from glory to glory

What's inside us always comes out. Jesus says so when He tells us that the mouth speaks from that which fills the heart.[2] Paul is staying on topic when he says from glory to glory. He's saying that the glory that we are is going to work itself out into the rest of our lives.

Glory isn't made to be bottled up in some hidden place: inner splendor would be wasted if it didn't show up in the way we live. We can relax. God doesn't waste inner glory; He makes it appear in real actions and real attitudes. The glory that we are inevitably seeps into the rest of our lives. Some of us may allow more seepage than others, but glory never remains a dark and total secret.

Glory changes the way we treat people, renews our thought life, and shapes our feelings. Gradually, but predictably, glory makes our character increasingly and poignantly beautiful. Self-centeredness gives way to love, just like God said it should. We actually start loving "somebody besides me."

But we need to keep the sequence straight: behavioral change follows self change. We get it backwards and think that if we do enough good things we'll become better people. Not true. Behavior doesn't change self. Self is changed first; behavioral improvements follow.

> *Behavior doesn't change self. Self changes behavior.*

The phrase "from glory to glory" promises this ongoing transformation – from glory already there to glory yet to develop. This really does happen. I've been a Christian for over 30 years. One of the benefits of having all those Christian years under my belt is the encouragement I get when I look back (with some chagrin) at my life a decade or three ago. My life has changed. Those around me can see signs of the out-workings of inner glory. I can too. I actually am being conformed to Jesus. And even though I'm only part way there, I'm no longer at the beginning of my journey.

Substantial change does happen this side of heaven – substantial change, not complete change. We'll have to wait until we meet Jesus face-to-face for the end of the process. Someday the work progressing inside us will be completed. Someday. Then, but not yet, the glory that already characterizes *us* will characterize everything we think, feel, and do. Someday everything about us will perfectly match who we are on the inside. What a relief. How reassuring. Someday actually comes.

Phrase 5: from the Lord the Spirit
Consider one last phrase from 2 Corinthians 3:18: *from the Lord the Spirit* and notice who is doing the transformation – not us, but the Spirit. Change is not up to us. This is important. Even if you're finally convinced that God has changed your inner being, I'll bet you still think it's your job to take charge and start improving your tasteless thoughts, eliminate your nasty emotions, and stifle your selfish desires. It's not. We aren't adequate to that task.

The God who changed us from dead to alive and from old to new also changes how we live. We don't have the ability to pull off more than superficial behavioral change. Deep transformation, change from the inside out, is the work of the Holy Spirit. Only He is adequate to conform us to God's character.[3]

Notes

Chapter 18 – Pirates, Mirrors, and Glory

1. The Greek phrase in 2 Corinthians 3:18, *ten doksan kuriou*, puts the word *Lord* in the genitive case. A genitive commonly connotes *possession*. If that were the issue here, the Greek phrase would translate *of the Lord*. I'm suggesting another choice. I believe that the genitive in this verse connotes *source* and should be translated *from the Lord*. It's an accepted grammatical choice, and better fits the logic of the verse: God has given glory *from* Himself *to* us.

2. *Luke 6:45 The good man out of the good treasure of his heart brings forth what is good; and the evil man out of the evil treasure brings forth what is evil; for his mouth speaks from that which fills his heart.*

3. *2 Corinthians 3:4 And such confidence we have through Christ toward God. 5 Not that we are adequate in ourselves to consider anything as coming from ourselves, but our adequacy is from God, 6 who also made us adequate as servants of a new covenant, not of the letter, but of the Spirit; for the letter kills, but the Spirit gives life.*

   This is God's promise to us.

19
Expectations and Exhaustion

You may have been agreeing with me (at least in an academic, theoretical sort of way) that God produces our glory, but is that your actual take on the situation? Not likely. As I've said, most Christians truly believe they're ugly inside and must work hard, very hard, to become like God. This belief accounts for why so many of us get discouraged, even exhausted, when we try to live out what we believe. It also explains why so many of us distance from our faith: we wear ourselves out trying to make ourselves acceptable to God.

Exhausted, worn out, and discouraged – terrible results, considering that becoming a Christian is supposed to bring us rest, even joy. If those of us who believe in Christ don't believe He's done anything to change us – and I'm not talking about minor adjustments, I'm talking about glorious deep-level change – we're stuck with trying to produce an acceptable self on our own. But if God has changed us, has changed *you*, what then? What if you, not because of your efforts but simply because of who you are, bring God rich pleasure?

EXPECTATIONS REVEALED

A few of you may think I'm being far too negative about your self-concept; you're sure you have a pretty good self-image. Let's test that out. Look again at 2 Corinthians 3:18.

> *But we all, with unveiled face, beholding as in a mirror the glory of the Lord, are being transformed into the same image from glory to glory, just as from the Lord, the Spirit.*

I've read a slightly altered version of this verse to a lot of people, and even though I have them look at the actual text while I read, no one so far has caught my intentional error. My phony version goes like this: "But we all, with unveiled face, beholding as in a mirror the glory of the Lord, are being changed into the same image from ugliness to glory, just as from the Lord, the Spirit."

People who think they're ugly inside accept my distortion as gospel truth. That you would expect. But – and here's what's odd – so do people who claim comfort with who they are. That *is* odd. Did you catch the word I changed? People don't start out their Christian life with an ugly inner self. They just think they do.

It's easy to fool someone if you tell them a lie that closely matches their own beliefs. People, so far without exception, expect me to say "ugliness," and when I do, a door closes in their minds. They may as well have closed their eyes. The letters forming the word "glory" on the page simply fade out of sight, erased by each individual's deep-rooted convictions. Strong opinions, especially when not acknowledged, effectively blind people to reality.

AGREEING WITH GOD

You've probably been blinded too. Be truthful with yourself. Don't
you assume that any semblance of glory is a long way off? And
aren't you at best hesitant to identify with glory?
Thinking we're glorious this side of heaven
sounds about as arrogant as the idea of being
complete, Maybe when I get to heaven I'll be
glorious. Really? If you think that way you're
contradicting God. You are. You're telling Him
He's a liar. That takes a lot of nerve.

> *To say "I'm glorious"*
> *only seems arrogant.*
> *Real arrogance is*
> *contradicting God.*

Still, considering various character flaws (from pride to sneaking
the last cookie) which of us would even think of using the word
glory to describe ourselves? I would. And not from ignorance about
my self-centeredness or from arrogance about my moral superiority,
but because I can't get up the moxie to contradict God.

Do you still find yourself resisting God on this point? Are you
feeling unworthy to even meet His eyes, much less look Him
straight in the face, and thank Him for making you glorious? It
does seem like a pushy, arrogant thing to do, but I don't believe it
is. I think real arrogance is a willingness to flat out contradict God.

We need humility. And it takes a scary amount of humility to
embrace a gift we in no way deserve. Identifying with glory turns
out to be harder than embracing shame. Be that as it may, we're
going to have to get used to it, because glory is true.

TRUSTING THE PRESENCE OF GLORY

Glory is true, but trusting in it produces a reasonable amount of
discomfort. Besides our internal worry that we might have made
a false claim, we're going to encounter a few setbacks from others

when we start to identify with glory. Think of the looks we'd encounter if we announced to our friends and neighbors that we were a glorious being, shining with inner wonder.

And of course there's also the self-imposed pressure of claiming glory and deciding we have to work really hard to keep it from slipping away. Also the problem of claiming glory and then having to explain to our friends why everything we do doesn't exactly match who we are claiming to be. Yet in spite of all these difficulties, glory remains true. We must learn to trust in it and embrace it without shame or apology.

PRODUCING TRUST

How do we produce such radical trust? The short answer is that we can't, because we can't force ourselves to believe anything, no matter how much we want to believe and no matter how hard we try. None of our efforts to change our mind about who we are will ever work. We can't make ourselves trust that we're new creations, and other people can't make us trust it either. It takes God to convince us of reality.

Years ago a Christian friend of mine kept going on and on about how she adored this married man. Her fantasy life, hopes, ideas – all of them about him – were running wild. I was impressed with her diligence as she tried to figure out how to make her dreams of life with him come true, but dismayed that the concept of his being off-limits didn't even register. She really, seriously liked him. Several of her friends, including me, would tell her, "Hey, he's married," and see no recognizing flicker in her eyes. Nothing. She'd say, once again, "I know; he's married," and then fill us in on her latest plans to get together with him.

I'd just about given up when one day the two of us met and she looked closely at me, paused, and said, "He's married." "Yes," I said, "He is." Subject closed. Our words had had no effect on her. But then the Lord touched her and made the truth click. It was a miracle, it really was, just like when Jesus healed the deaf and the blind and the ignorant.

MAKING THE TRUTH CLICK

Making the truth click is where the Holy Spirit comes in. The Bible says the Spirit will guide us into all truth.[1] We need a guide, because we can't get to truth by ourselves. We can stare at the pages of the Bible for unbelievably long periods of time and remain just as unconvinced that the words on the pages are true as when we started reading. God has given us this wonderful written mirror that reveals our glory, yet when we read His words they just don't click. This is incredibly frustrating. And discouraging.

We simply don't have the ability to flip a switch in our minds that turns God's truth from abstract to real. Then how does truth get transferred from our minds to our hearts? Not by us, but by the Spirit. We have to wait for Him to act.

I'm speaking from personal experience. I can't make myself believe in anything – producing faith is beyond my grasp. When someone tells me "You just have to have faith!" it grates on my nerves.

> *I can't make myself believe in anything – producing faith is beyond my grasp.*

Do they think I could generate faith if I got serious and actually worked at it? "You have to have faith" reeks with the suggestion that I'm failing to do something I really could do if I only tried harder.

It feels like a putdown. I get mad. I know I need more faith; just don't tell me that I ought to be able to produce it. I can't. (If those other people stopped paying attention to my lack of ability they'd discover they're no better at producing faith than I am.)

Faith, belief, trust – whatever you call it – doesn't come through willpower or human effort, ours or anybody else's. Our failed attempts to force ourselves (or pressure others) to trust God make that pretty obvious. At a minimum, this is disheartening, at least it is until the Spirit makes another truth click: it's not up to us to make faith happen. God makes faith happen. All by Himself. In His own time. We don't have the ability to produce faith, in ourselves or in others.

I didn't used to think this way. I used to think I could change what other people believed. Before my husband came to know the Lord I'd sometimes read the Bible to Him while he was taking a shower. I'd stand just outside the frosted glass door and talk loudly so I could be heard over the running water, and the beauty of the event was that there was no way he could escape. I was being totally obnoxious. When my husband was later drawn to Jesus, the Spirit worked through someone other than me, someone a little less pushy.

This all happened years ago, giving me time to learn about backing off from responsibilities that aren't mine. I've found that I can't create faith and that I'm not responsible to do so, either inside my own brain or over the shower door. Neither can you. Only God creates faith. When we try to produce it in ourselves or in others we're taking over God's responsibilities. That's sinful. And foolish. Making the truth click is God's job. It's the work of God the Spirit.

OUR PART

Still, we do have a part in believing God, two parts actually. First, we need to become familiar with what He's already written to us, and second, we need to ask Him to help us believe what we've read. The first part is reading the Bible; the second part is pleading with Him to give us faith in its words. The two go together.

Knowing personally what the Bible says is crucial. We can listen to people tell us about His message, but there's no substitute for a firsthand encounter with the text. If we ask, the same Spirit who was breathed into us will breathe reality into the words we read. He will open our eyes to what's on the page, reveal to us how God thinks, and woo our hearts with descriptions of what it's like to be His intimate. The whole process is strangely amazing. It's another miracle.

Some of God's words are easier to swallow than others. Most of our unbelief in what He says stems from our allegiance to our own personal agendas. When His message touches an area of our life we'd rather not change, His words don't sound even remotely plausible. But, if we can get up the courage, we can ask Him to change our resistance. To melt our unbelief.

In Mark 9, the father of a demon-possessed by cried out to Jesus, *Help my unbelief!* [2] His cry is precisely the place to start and perhaps the last thing we want to pray. Unlike the father, we think if we admit our unbelief to God He'll get mad instead of offering us help. That's not what happens. Going to God with our struggles doesn't cut us off from Him but draws us near. Of course it does.

We and God share the same desire: we both want to get rid of unbelief, not perpetuate it. This righteous plea – *Help my unbelief!* – warms God's heart.

Unbelief is not our responsibility. Really. We don't have to fix unbelief; we just need to call for God's help. *"I do believe; help my unbelief."* Producing faith is the work of God - the Son and the Holy Spirit and the Father. Jesus begins faith in the first place and expands it until it's complete.[3] The Holy Spirit makes the truth click, transfers it from our heads to our hearts, and convinces us that what the Father has said is actually true. It happens regularly, just like with my infatuated friend. Producing faith is the work of God.

Faith resolves a lot of issues; for starters, it convinces us that God is telling us the truth. Faith makes us believe what we see and have doubted, believe what we hear and have discarded, and believe even when what we can see seems to contradict what He says. Sometimes faith happens slowly – truth may take some time to come into focus. Still, whether the faith you need develops over a long time or comes suddenly, it will happen. That you can trust.

Our part is asking God for help. We won't get a Seeing Eye dog or a red tipped cane, but our Lord will touch our eyes and make us sure of crucial invisible realities – like who He is, and who we are.

The ophthalmologist from above gives us new eyes – eyes of faith. But we still need to learn how to use them. Specifically, we must learn where to look. We have to shift our focus.

NOTES

CHAPTER 19 – EXPECTATIONS AND EXHAUSTION

1. *John 16:13 But when He, the Spirit of truth, comes, He will guide you into all the truth; for He will not speak on His own initiative, but whatever He hears, He will speak; and He will disclose to you what is to come.*

2. *Mark 9:17 And one of the crowd answered Him, "Teacher, I brought You my son, possessed with a spirit which makes him mute;..." 21 And He asked his father, "How long has this been happening to him?" And he said, "From childhood. 22 And it has often thrown him both into the fire and into the water to destroy him. But if You can do anything, take pity on us and help us!" 23 And Jesus said to him, "If You can! All things are possible to him who believes." 24 Immediately the boy's father cried out and began saying, "I do believe; help my unbelief."*

3. *Hebrews 12:2 fixing our eyes on Jesus, the author and perfecter of faith...*

20
Double Vision, Single Self

I remember my father-in-law's prism glasses. He'd been seeing double images – two dogs, two leashes, two fire hydrants. His doctor fixed the problem by prescribing glasses with custom made prism lenses. The prisms bent the incoming light rays so, wonder of wonders, he ended up seeing one dog, one leash, and one fire hydrant. No more double vision. Quite an improvement.

Double vision on a spiritual level is a more serious problem. Instead of a second illusory dog, we see a second illusory self, one that unsettles us. Enough attention to this second self convinces most of us that we're failures and makes us wary even to hope we might have inherent value. What is this illusory second self we keep seeing? The Bible calls it our "flesh."

141

FLESH DEFINED

You may have heard about flesh, but you're probably slightly fuzzy about defining it. What exactly is flesh?

Sometimes when a Bible writer says flesh it's easy to tell that he means our physical bodies, stuff like knees and noses and curly hair. That's the physical flesh. It's visible and it's good.

Sometimes, however, the writer strikes a darker chord and warns about flesh of another kind: spiritual flesh. Spiritual flesh worms its way into our souls, twists our thinking, agitates our responses, and can turn our stomach at its touch. This is the kind of flesh I'm talking about here.

Flesh, simply stated, is our knee-jerk resistance to God, our innate inclination to oppose Him. It motivates us to contradict God. It urges us to substitute our will for His and operate without listening to His voice. Flesh incites rebellion against God. Consider it our inside source of the rotten things we do.

FOCUSED ON OUR FLESH

Sadly, many of us give our flesh a lot of attention. Even though we can't see our God-like exquisiteness, we aren't totally devoid of vision – we're quite skilled at noticing each ungodly thing we do. Though we try and see what's good about us, we end up focused on things quite the opposite.

Our present experience isn't the only bad news. Past screw-ups, like scenes from a personal horror movie, can instantly be brought to mind. Even worse, neither past nor present experiences encourage us to anticipate a better future. We may have a lot of trouble noticing the presence of the awesome. But seeing the appalling? That's easy. We are keen (though reluctant) observers of our failures. Glaring in the foreground are the very deeds we prefer to keep out of sight, the attitudes we'd rather not notice, the unsolicited thoughts that surface and dismay us. Again and again we look at our flesh and at its product, sin. (Think of sin as flesh acting out.)

Reacting to the junk

We respond in a variety of ways when faced with our fleshly misdeeds. Some of us groan in despair: *How could I have done that ... again? I'll never change.* Others, particularly those with less courage (or less masochism), tune out and become indifferent: they ignore the evidence of their failings. A few take a more extreme step and twist the ugly until it takes on a perverse attraction. And, most destructive of all, almost everyone assumes that the junk we see is who we are. Most of us identify with our flesh.

Despair. Indifference. Attraction. Identification. Each of these reactions to seeing our flesh is a toxic choice nurtured by a seemingly harmless pastime: introspection.

INTROSPECTION UNMASKED

Everybody knows about introspection. We all focus inwardly to try and glimpse who we are and rate how we're doing. You may be fond of introspection. I'm not much of a fan.

Introspection teases us with the promise of self-knowledge. We shouldn't believe that promise. Introspection won't tell us who we are; introspection only tells us who we aren't. That glance inside doesn't show us self, it only shows us our flesh, and therein lies the problem. For a Christian, flesh is dead, and when we focus on the flesh we feel dead too. Introspection really ought to be called morbid introspection, because it's a deadly practice.

> *Introspection only tells us who we aren't.*

FLESH REVEALED

We all are quite familiar with our flesh. Even the spiritually lifeless see enough evidence of warped thoughts and selfish behavior to remind them that something about *them* is seriously wrong. The Bible calls this wrongness "flesh." For unbelievers, flesh is who they are. They are, by nature, fleshly. For unbelievers, identifying with the flesh reflects the truth.

Not so for believers. For those of us who have accepted Jesus as our Lord, our basic identity has changed – from fleshly to righteous. Flesh no longer describes our nature but has become simply one more of our possessions. Look at Ephesians 2:3.

> *Among them [unbelievers] we [believers] too all formerly lived in the lusts of **our** flesh, indulging the desires of the flesh and of the mind, and **were** by nature children of wrath, even as the rest.*

Look carefully at Paul's words: He says *our* flesh. Ours. What used to be us has become ours, just one more thing we have. In chapter 10, I differentiated what we have from who we are. Paul has just called flesh another of our possessions. Flesh is *ours* but not *us*.

Flesh is no more us than is our car or our watch. You may stumble a bit with this idea, since it feels much more awkward to differentiate self from your flesh than it does to differentiate self from your other stuff. But the distinction is crucial. You're (hopefully) sure that you aren't your car. I want you to be even more sure that you aren't your flesh. Flesh is just one more thing that you have. Put flesh into the "stuff is not self" category.

Look at Paul's words again: we *were* by nature children of wrath, fleshly children. We *were*. The past tense is important. Christians must not continue to identify with their pre-Christian nature.

At the moment of salvation, Christ creates in us a new nature. *If anyone is in Christ he is a **new** creation* (2 Corinthians 5:17). New as in never before seen, new as in no longer fleshly. Flesh used to be us. But no longer.

A UNIQUELY CHRISTIAN PROBLEM

The visibility of our flesh gets more vivid when we become alive in Jesus – unbelievers see only signs of the flesh, but believers? We see flesh directly and see it with a clarity that makes our toenails curl backwards.

We can see our flesh because it's not us. Think back to the one-eyed pirate with sand in his eye. His eye couldn't see itself; it could only see other things. "I's" can't see themselves either ... but they can see other things. Those of us transformed by Jesus can see our flesh because it's become one of those other things. Flesh is no longer us, but *ours* (Ephesians 2:3). *We* are new creations (2 Corinthians 5:17).

Our ability to see our flesh ought to deeply reassure us. The fact that flesh is so visible should produce confidence that flesh is no longer us. Confidence, rejoicing, relief, and thanksgiving.

But if you're like most people that hasn't been your reaction. When you see your flesh, you feel like pond scum. Years of rebelling against God, followed by more years of focusing on your sins, have confirmed your belief that you're ugly inside. You assume that what you see is who you are; you look at your flesh and then you identify with it. That's a terrible choice – identifying with our flesh twists our choices, thoughts, and feelings into macabre caricatures of the truth. It happens every time we confuse flesh with self.

Many of us think that God also confuses flesh with self. We think God identifies us with our flesh and never embrace the reality that

He delights in us. Considering what we do, how could He possibly find us wonderful? We're missing the fact that His anger is not at us but at our sin.

Think of it this way: we only cry over what is dear to our hearts. Jesus mourned over Jerusalem[1] because each person in that city, even those who rejected Him, was dear to His heart. Jesus also weeps when any of us, Christian or not, fall short of what we could be. His eyes fill with tears when we waste the beauty He has built into each of us. His heart breaks when anyone rejects His offer of life.

The Lord delights in what He has created. Alive or dead, He values us all. He sees behind our failings to our inherent dignity.

PRISM GLASSES FROM GOD

God always disconnects flesh from worth. For Christians, He also disconnects flesh from self. You would think this fact would bring believers immense relief. It generally doesn't.

Why not? Because of our double-vision. Instead of two dogs and two fire hydrants, Christians see two "selves" standing side by side, and we don't know which one is really us. In the Bible, we see a new glorious self, but our lives, repeatedly, show a different story. In our lives, we keep failing, decide that our failures negate God's good news, and identify with shame instead of glory.

We don't grasp the truth that we are glorious beings, beings who *have* flesh and *act* sinfully, beings who are by nature neither fleshly nor sinful. Instead, we describe ourselves as sinners through and through. Bad choice. We aren't what we have and we aren't what we do and we aren't what other people say we are. We, by God's gift, are glorious.

Are you having trouble believing this? God will help. He provides the prism glasses that rid us of double vision and allow us to see who we really are. He writes his prescription in Romans 7:17 and 7:20. We'll look there next.

NOTES

CHAPTER 20 – DOUBLE VISION, SINGLE SELF

1. *Matthew 23:37 O Jerusalem, Jerusalem, who kills the prophets and stones those who are sent to her! How often I wanted to gather your children together, the way a hen gathers her chicks under her wings, and you were unwilling.*

    Jesus' heart broke when He saw the unwillingness of the people in Jerusalem to accept Him. You may not think you have that kind of impact on Him. Are you aware that you can break His heart?

21
Not Self but Sin

Most Christians not only identify with their fleshly inclinations but identify also with the sin their flesh exudes. But look at the truth: Paul emphatically separates self from sin:

> *Romans 7:17 So now **no longer am I** the one doing it, **but sin** which dwells **in me**.*

> *Romans 7:20 But if I am doing the very thing I do not want, **I am no longer** the one doing it, **but sin** which dwells **in me**.*

No longer I, but sin in me. I no longer, but sin in me. Paul says it twice to hammer home his point: there is a complete disconnect between identity and evil. Sin (the product of flesh) no longer reveals what we are; it only reveals what we were. Don't skip over that last sentence; it's foundational. A Christian's identity is no longer defined by sin.[1]

Not only does sin no longer define believers, neither do its relatives, flesh and death. I say relatives, because these three (flesh, sin, and death) form a grisly sort of three generational family: flesh is the father of sin and sin is the father of death. We used to be identified as members of this family – fleshly, sinful, and dead. But no longer. Now we take after Jesus; we've become members of His family. Our old family may still live nearby, but they no longer identify who we are; we no longer share their family tree.

> *Flesh, sin, and death may still be **in** us, but they no longer **are** us.*

SHIFTING FROM DEATH TO LIFE

This whole idea of being righteous (having sin, but not being sin) is so counterintuitive that we balk at Paul's clear meaning. We've become so certain that we're sinful to the core that it's almost beyond our ability to think of being a self cleansed from that stain. But we can, and we must, allow Paul's point to penetrate our mental roadblocks. Paul is telling us the truth: self is not fleshly nor sinful nor dead.

Paul's point is easier to understand if we think of human life as a sequence of stages: first physical birth, second (hopefully) spiritual birth, followed by the third stage, heavenly life.

First comes a physical birth; the new baby starts out physically alive, but (and here's the human tragedy) spiritually dead. The Bible identifies us with our spiritual state and calls those in this phase "dead." That's their identity. Unlike Adam and Eve who started out alive and shifted to dead, we start out dead. Physical decline is built into a baby's genes, and spiritual death already has staked its claim. We begin our lives as image bearers with a disability: physically limited and spiritually lifeless. Fleshly by nature. That's Stage #1.

Stage #1 can last forever, but it doesn't have to. When we yield ourselves to Jesus, He changes our spiritual deadness to spiritual life. After this spiritual birth, we're alive physically *and* spiritually. The Bible (again using our spiritual state to identify who we are) calls everyone in this second stage "alive." We become living spiritual beings, new creations with a new identity.

A new identity! Marvelous – but not without troubles. Though new, we remain stuck, not only with the presence of that unwelcome trio (flesh, sin, and death) but also with its perpetrator, the Evil One. We spend this post-Christian pre-heaven portion of our lives in the presence of our enemies. This is Stage #2.

Entrance into Stage #2 guarantees a future entrance into Stage #3, heavenly life. At the time of physical death, the already spiritually alive get new living bodies that match their already living selves. In this last stage three heavenly life begins and continues forever. That's truly good news.

If you're one of the living ones, entering heaven guarantees a permanent exit from the deadly trio and their deadly instigator. In heaven only God's glory remains. Heaven is what we've been groaning and longing for the entire time we've been on earth.

In a diagram, the stages look like this:

Side by Side: The Old and the New

"I" = an old dead spiritual being	the flesh = no longer "I"	
	"I" = a new living spiritual being	"I" = a new living spiritual being
#1_____ **Physical Birth**	#2 _____ **Spiritual Birth**	#3 _____ **Heavenly Life**

How does all this work out practically? Let's look at the stages in more detail.

STAGE #1: PHYSICAL BIRTH

When were you born? Put that date in the diagram after #1. That's when you came into the world, physically alive but spiritually dead.

The New Testament uses various words, all negative, to typify this part of your life: dead, old, former, sinful, fleshly. All these words point to glaring flaws that accompany the absence of the breath of God. The only way to disconnect yourself from these flaws is to join yourself to Jesus.

STAGE #2: SPIRITUAL BIRTH

When did you yield your life to Jesus? Fill that date in after #2 (an approximate date is fine, you just need to know that it's happened). At the moment you yielded to Him you got a *new* identity. (Remember this word "new" – we'll get back to it shortly).

Getting a new identity goes a long, long way, but we still have a problem – our flesh hasn't left, not yet, and neither has the sin it exudes. Though sin no longer is us, we still have to endure its presence. Flesh, sin, and death no longer remain our relatives, but they're still camping in the basement. From spiritual birth until our welcome into heaven, these old enemies dwell alongside the new glorious self. The two horizontal lines in the center section of the diagram show that simultaneous and frustrating coexistence.

Now be careful here. While the new and the old sit side by side, don't jump to the conclusion that they combine to make a self. We're not a duality with a split personality. Two sets of traits are present, but only one is our nature – the other is our burden.

The continued presence of the old is difficult to
bear. Who wants minute-by-minute reminders of
their failures? The reminders are bad enough, but
even worse, the presence of the old causes a lot of
confusion. It is incredibly hard to keep in mind

*Flesh, sin, and death,
are still camping
in the basement.*

that we aren't the same as the flesh we keep encountering.

Encounter by a graveyard

I've experienced this encounter first-hand. I'd just taught a class
badly – screwed up my priorities, winged my preparation, and
counted on native skill to get me through. It was humiliating. I
felt like a fool. On my way home I pulled the car over on a hillside
overlooking a graveyard, the perfect place to match my mood.
The Lord kept telling me to pay attention to what had just
happened, but I kept avoiding the misery. He persisted, and I
balked. We went back and forth for about half an hour until I
finally yielded and revisited the embarrassing event.

What happened next caught me by surprise: I suddenly realized
that I wasn't the same as that flesh from which I was recoiling. I
observed my flesh; I cringed at my flesh, but I hadn't *become* my
flesh. I had simply failed to act consistently with who I was. The
truth had clicked: the old wasn't me, it was just my burden. Doing
a jerky thing hadn't transformed me into a jerk. I wasn't the same
as the flesh, sin, and death I'd encountered. The old was just the
old. And I was a new creation in Christ. What an incredible relief.
Thank God.

With newfound freedom, I repented of my irresponsibility and
rejoiced in my dignity, the exact things God wanted me to do. It
was wonderful. The old was just the old. And I was new.

New

The word "new" highlights the great divide between flesh and self. You already know that life and completeness (and all the rest) have made us remarkably different from who we were. You may not appreciate the immensity of the change that "new" implies. When Paul says "new creation" and when I say "new identity," we both are emphasizing a shift that makes us amazingly different from who we were before we met Jesus.

The Greek of the original New Testament uses two different words for new, each with a unique emphasis. One word for new, *neos*,[2] means recent in time. Luke uses that word when he tells us about new wine bursting old wineskins.[3] But when Paul tells us we are new creations,[4] he uses the other word for new, *kainos*,[4] a startling word. *Kainos* describes something that *never before existed*. Paul's use of this word assures us that we are altogether different from what we were before. *Kainos* emphasizes the totality of our identity change.

You should take a moment to ponder this; the implications are so obvious that they're easy to overlook. Something never before experienced has to be different from what's already known. The uniquely new can't be the same as the familiar old. The sinful flesh, well-known and familiar, used to be us. But no longer. We are no longer the old – we're new. Our old identity hasn't evolved; it's been replaced.

> *Our old identity hasn't evolved; it's been replaced.*

I'm not saying that Christians don't sin – clearly we do. And I'm not saying that we aren't responsible to turn away from sin – clearly we are. But sin now grates against the cleanness and purity of the new us. What used to be comfortable has become alien.

Sin remains present, but it no longer describes self, not if we're alive in Christ. A gigantic and permanent divide has been created between who we really are and our sin-producing flesh. If you think that every wrong thing you do (or have done) defines you, you need some new thoughts.

Sin, handcuffed to flesh, is no longer our identity. It's not us. It used to be us, but that's changed. Make sure you differentiate both of these lingering invaders from who you now are. Flesh is no more than something we have, and sin is no more than something we do. Think of flesh as stuff and sin as an activity; just don't confuse either one with your identity.

STAGE #3: HEAVENLY BIRTH

This is the last part of the story, the part that never ends. Eternity goes on forever. Our earthly bodies don't.

I'm writing these words on my birthday. Each year I "mature" (my new word for growing old), I learn a bit more vividly that my body isn't going to last forever. At some point I, and you, will physically die. Since we don't know when the event will take place, you'll have to fill in the blank after stage #3 with a question mark.

Even though the timing is uncertain, we do know that this last stage brings believers a mind-boggling release. In heaven the flesh that produces sin will be history, the death that follows sin will have disappeared, and the enemy spirit behind flesh, sin, and death will be permanently banished from our presence. When we leave our earthly bodies and step into heavenly ones, our present struggle with the enemies camping in the basement will be history.

Helen's story

My friend Helen knows that earthly enemies are heavenly history.
She found out right before she died. One day we were chatting,
when Helen offhandedly mentioned she really wasn't looking
forward to heaven.

"Why not?" I asked.

"Well, it's just more of the same struggle we have here."

"No, no," I said, "Heaven is different." And I told her about
no more flesh and no more sin and no more death.

"You mean all the crap will be gone?!" She could hardly believe it.

"Completely gone." As I spoke I smiled, and her joy filled the
room.

Helen hadn't known she was ill, but four days later she died and
left all the crap behind. I smile again as I imagine her current
unedited praise of the wonder of life unspoiled by crap. Now she
knows heaven firsthand. Where Helen now lives everything is
without flaw.

Without flaw. That's going to feel weird, almost surreal – we're
so used to living with flesh, sin, and death that heaven will feel
strange. But strange in a good way. Strange with wonder and
strange with joy. Heaven will be strange, yet hauntingly familiar.
At first glance we'll recognize all those things we knew this earth
was missing. As the new Eden springs into focus, we'll exult,
"At last!" This ruined earth scrapes our skin; heaven will have a
delicious touch. Heaven fits us – we are, after all, designed to live
in a paradise. And we have not yet reached our destination.

WARY OF RISK

Because the continued presence of flesh, sin, and death makes it
so difficult to believe we have a new identity, we're tempted to

treat the presence of a new self as a fairy tale — great ending but no substance. No matter how deeply we want inner glory to be real, trusting its actual presence is a stretch. We feel cautious.

Counting on the words of an invisible God seems like a huge risk. What if the new self He describes isn't there and we're proved a fool? What if we've been duped, and we're not new after all? What if we claim to be different inside and are exposed as unchanged?

We've all been shamed and have learned well to guard ourselves from repeating the experience. At times, masks lowered and guard down, we act spontaneously. Yet even in these moments we don't quite let go of our watchfulness; we worry that, instead of glory, something uglier might appear. Few of us are comfortable being in the spotlight.

Fear of personal exposure is only one of our problems. Fear of having the rug pulled out from under our hopes is another. What if we count on this gift that holds such joy and discover there's nothing there? Perhaps it's better not to hope at all, better to play it safe and doubt that we're new.

Os Guinness expresses our caution perfectly when he explains what he calls "doubting for joy."[6]

> Healthy faith can be pictured as the firm, solid grip of a person who is able to reach out and grasp whatever he or she wants to hold. Imagine what it would be like, though, to grasp something firmly if you had a bad wound in the palm of your hand.... This is what happens [with] this kind of doubt. People know they need the truth in question; they can see the difference it would make; they can even see that it is true; and

they are quite able to believe it. The problem is that the very process of believing puts painful pressure on old psychological wounds…. When this happens, doubt is the…excuse for drawing back from such a risk.

Guinness illustrates his point by describing the disciples' reaction when Jesus appears to them the evening of Resurrection Sunday.

Without warning, Jesus suddenly entered the room where his disciples were assembled and confronted them with the living reality of his risen presence. Momentarily they were taken aback, caught in two minds over whether to believe, and Luke captures the curious suspension of that moment: "And while they still disbelieved for joy…" (Luke 24:41)

What they were seeing was the one thing in all the world they wanted most. That was precisely the trouble. They wanted it so much that to believe it and then discover it was false would have been profoundly disillusioning. So, instead, they preferred the safety of doubt rather than the risk of disappointment.

Guinness (via Luke) has precisely portrayed our motives. His words sound familiar, don't they? We've all vacillated between belief and unbelief in an effort to ward off the risk of a broken heart.

It seems like a no-brainer: keep the status quo and not take any risks. But if we take no risks? Then we'll be out of touch with God and robbed of knowing who we really are.

How can we become so sure of worth and glory that we're willing to depend on it? We need more than those new eyes the doctor gave us.

We're going to have to shift our focus.

NOTES
CHAPTER 21 – NOT SELF BUT SIN

1. I'm convinced that the "I" in Romans 7:14–25 refers to Paul
   as an individual Christian believer now separated from sin.
   My point about the separation of self from sin, however, is not
   dependant on this particular passage. Other passages, such 2
   Corinthians 5:17 (which refers to the presence of something
   altogether new), confirm the presence in believers of something
   different from the old pre-Christian self.

2. *Neos* means new, as in fresh, or young (e.g. new wine).

3. *Luke 5:3.*

4. *2 Corinthians 5:17. Kainos* means new in the sense of
   something previously unknown and unheard (e.g. a new self).

5. Os Guinness, *God in the Dark*, Crossway Books, Wheaton,
   Illinois, 1996, excerpts taken from pp. 146-149. I highly
   recommend this book. If you can, get your hands on its out-of-
   print predecessor (*In Two Minds*, IVP, 1977) which contains a
   section on counsel that is omitted from the second edition.

22

Double World, Single Focus

Morbidly introspecting. Scanning our activity. Inspecting our stuff.
Focusing on failure. Checking out our flesh. With eyes like these
it's a wonder we can find the sofa. We certainly can't find ourselves.
Our dilemma stems from where we're looking: everyplace except at
God.

When we rely on our own eyes to tell us who we are, we end up
with a stunningly deficient definition of self. We should rely on
the God who knows us well; we should shift our focus to what He
says about us. Trying to define ourselves has led to nothing but
heartbreak.

LOOKING AT THE EXCELLENT

Besides the heartbreak, there's another reason not to focus on all this ugliness – it's sinful. Really, it is. Focus on flesh is the opposite of where God tells us to look:

> *Philippians 4:8 Finally, brethren, whatever is true, whatever is honorable, whatever is right, whatever is pure, whatever is lovely, whatever is of good repute, if there is any excellence and if anything worthy of praise, let your mind dwell on these things.*

These things – honorable, pure, excellent and the like – are the antithesis of flesh, and these things must occupy our focus. Don't think that looking at the excellent is a stupid reality-avoiding mind-game. God is not asking us to ignore reality; He's asking us to concentrate on the excellent part of reality. Think of it this way: we're not paranoid if someone really is after us. And we're not ignoring reality if the excellent really is there.

Shifting our focus, from the ugly to the excellent or from the false to the true, is far from stupid and a long way from ignoring reality. When we shift our focus in the direction God suggests, we find, to our surprise, that our inner experience (like our perspective on who we are) shifts from discouraging to deeply joyful. Something so simple, just looking where God tells us to look, turns out to be something profound.

LOOKING TOWARD

I'm not telling you to simply look away from the fleshly junk. That doesn't work. Any shift in focus has to be twofold, looking away from one thing and at something else. Preferably away from our own ideas and towards God's.

Merely looking away is a lost cause. We all know this is true. When we try to look away from things, like lies about who we are, the lies linger at the edge of our awareness. But when we look towards something, like God, truth commands our attention. Lies fade away when we stop looking at them. We don't even notice that they have gone.

If you've ever dined at a mediocre Italian restaurant, you know how exactly how this works. You sit down and notice a basket lined with red and white checked gingham and filled with bread – yesterday's bread. A quick touch of its stale surface instantly prompts you to scan the room for a waiter to bring you fresh bread. When he finally brings a hot steaming loaf, everybody digs in. And nobody notices where the stale bread has gone. It might still be on the table. Who knows? Who cares? The new has commanded your attention.

God's truth is fresh bread. When He speaks, lies fade into the background and truth satiates our hunger. Read His words that affirm our value, reassure us of His presence, and tell us we're new. Shift your focus to Him, and the lies about your worth will fade away.

Focus on this: we all bear the invisible image of God. This alone is a solid basis for dignity, a reason to be certain of your worth. And focus on this: if Jesus is your Lord, you have been changed in a truly miraculous way – new life and glory have been added to your dignity. Jesus' breath, breathed in, has brought with it a new self, solid with worth and glory. God says so. Breathe in and agree with Him.

PART VI
Authenticity and Dignity

Part VI Overview
Authenticity and Dignity

How do we apply what we've been talking about? How do we start to live out who we are? That depends on whether we're spiritually alive or whether we're not.

How about you? Are you joined to Jesus or are you still living on your own? Either way the choices before you are profound.

Authenticity and Dignity, the final part of this book, lays out the practical and significant consequences of knowing who we are. Chapter 23, *Being Who We Are*, summarizes the profound influence that self (and our view of self) has on our thoughts, emotions, and choices. Chapter 24, *Being Me at the Airport*, details how the Lord carefully planned an overseas trip to teach the author how to move from the shame of humiliation into the glory of humility.

God gives life and glory. Will you embrace His gifts?

23
Being Who We Are

How do we appropriate what we've been talking about? How do we start to live out who we are? That depends on whether we're joined to Jesus or still living on our own.

WHEN WE'RE STILL ON OUR OWN

When I finally handed Jesus my life, I was bone-tired – weary of emptiness and exhausted by inner-turmoil. I hope you're bone-tired too, and starving for life.

You may think God's gift of life is too good to be true. There must be a catch – and there is. You don't get the gift without accepting the Giver as your Lord.

If you flinch at the idea of having a "Lord," you're certainly not alone. Rule, authority, lordship – such words push at a place in each of us that yells, "NO!" Resisting another's control is a deeply entrenched choice. Accepting Jesus as Lord looks like a radical and unsettling decision.

It is.

Jesus was my last card. Even thinking about handing Him the reins terrified me. My efforts to control my life had given me a semblance of self and a fragile sense of safety, but they fell far short of meeting my needs. None of them filled my inner emptiness or chased away my shame or eased my many fears. I had no joy in my life, and I was starving for joy. So I took the risk.

Do you think it's better not to risk? Better to try to dull your pain, ignore your nagging sense of emptiness, and avoid this unpredictable (yet enticing) God? Are you convinced it's wiser to hedge your bets and easier to pretend that joy isn't a big deal? You certainly can keep on trying, but you'll never succeed. Why? Because a hunger for real joy, deep joy, is built into each one of us – we can't get rid of it, and only God can satisfy it.

The built-in hunger for joy is, in reality, a built-in hunger for God. He's given us longings that can only be met by Him. If you're thinking this is a set up, you're right. But it also makes sense. After all, this joyous God made us like Himself. It follows without fail that when joy is absent we miss it terribly.

When I gave myself to God, His gift of life surprised me. I had hoped for relief – and I got it – but I never expected joy. I had no idea that God brought with Him such delight, or that I would find such pleasure in His company.

As Os Guinness pointed out, the disciples doubted for joy, fearing that they couldn't stand it if they reached toward the seemingly resurrected Jesus and came away with empty hands. Their fear of dashed hopes made them hesitate to believe in the very thing they wanted most.

How about you? Will you risk asking for the pleasure of His lordship? If you do, you won't be disappointed. He will restore life to your broken image and richness to your experiences. His offer calls for a response – positive or negative. You can't choose neutrality; ignoring this offer is the same as rejecting it.

Will you accept or will you refuse?

WHEN WE'RE JOINED TO JESUS

If Jesus is our Lord, then now, this side of heaven, God offers us some astonishing freedoms, freedoms that we've longed for most of our lives. There is, however, a catch: to experience these freedoms we must not just read about what God says, we must act on it.

Jesus makes this point impossible to miss:

> *Luke 6:46 And why do you call Me, "Lord, Lord," and do not do what I say? 47 Everyone who comes to Me, and* **hears My words, and acts upon them,** *I will show you whom he is like: 48 he is like a man building a house, who dug deep and* **laid a foundation upon the rock,** *and when a flood rose, the torrent burst against that house and could not shake it, because it had been well built. 49 But the one who has* **heard, and has not acted** *accordingly, is like a man who built a house upon the ground* **without any foundation;** *and the torrent burst against it and immediately it collapsed, and the ruin of that house was great.*

His words apply to us. If we listens to God's truth but don't act
on it, our efforts will fall apart. We (the person inside) won't be
destroyed but our life will contain so many empty places. But if we
follow through? Then we're on rock-solid ground. The empty places
will be filled.

How about you? Are you willing to act on what God says about
who you are? Are you willing to build your identity on a dependable
foundation? God is our rock.[1] So are His words. He bids us to cling
to Him[2] as we venture into a new way of living.

BEING NEW – SOME PRACTICAL GUIDELINES

How different our lives would look if our beliefs and behavior
matched who we are. As new creations we are free to do some
wonderful things. We can, for example:

Stop pretending

Walter Mitty never learned to feel good without his fantasies. But
we don't need fantasies. We have what Walter was missing: a real
God who tells us the truth about our value. Our search is over.

Notice "somebody besides me"

With the issue of identity settled, we no longer have to be self-
centered and absorbed with our own value. We can get over
ourselves and notice what's going on outside of ourselves. We can
value God. We can even value our neighbors.

Stop trying to hide

We no longer need to squirm when we're called to the front of the
room. Being scrutinized, even criticized, poses no threat. Finally we
can live openly – without fig-leaves or masks. Without hypocrisy.
At our core we are living and glorious, and there is no longer any
reason to hide in shame. At last it's safe to step into the spotlight.

Identify with God

We're made in the image of the Spirit-Wind-Breath-like God, and we're like Him: valuable yet invisible, invisible yet knowable, recognized but not seen. Self is present; it's just not physical. Self is spiritual. Just like God. We can identify with Him.

Stop identifying with what we have

That Harley guy used the visible to feel valuable. He thought that lots of chrome upped his standing as a human being. We don't have to imitate him. Stuff, absent or present, doesn't change who we are. I need to remember that when I'm driving around in my sporty convertible. Stuff is not self. What is ours is not us.

Stop identifying with what we do

My baby's pediatrician would have enjoyed my company a lot more if I'd learned this before we met. Who knows, I might even have said "Thanks," when he called me Mom. You don't have to imitate me. Activity isn't identity; none of what we do changes *us*. I need to remember that when I start depending on my role for my worth. God never lets our activity alter our identity.

Stop letting people tell us who we are

Other people rarely, if ever, see us accurately. We can't even figure out our own identity. Only God sees us clearly, breathes us a glorious new self, and loves us enough to tell us who we really are.

Stop comparing ourselves with others

Our worth is unrelated to what others have, what they do, or what they think.

Feel God's touch

We started our time on earth unaroused by God's touch, His words, or His love. Our spiritual senses were calloused and unfeeling and God's touch didn't excite us. But God changed all that. Our magnificent and generous Lover deliberately and powerfully awakened our deadened senses. Unexpectedly and with authority He has rescued us from death and aroused us to Himself. Now we can tremble with joy at His touch.

Delight in who we are

When we accept God's wooing our very identity is altered. Who are we after we've breathed in God's life? We are living spiritual beings, created by God in His likeness and image, transformed by God's breath, dwelling in earthen vessels, and made into new creations who are complete in Him. Like overflowing sponges, we have been filled with Him. There are no empty, or ugly, spaces in self.

Accept God's delight in who we are

God sees us as new creations. Though He deeply loves and values each person on earth, His delight soars when the people He has created embrace His presence.

Perceive glory

We can use God's mirror, His word, to show us what we can't directly see. He's brought shine to His tarnished image-bearers; He's breathed glory into us. We can sense that glory. We can even be at ease with that glory, because glory is true.

Focus on the new

No more prism glasses. No more spiritual double vision. No more slavery to a focus on flesh, sin, and death. No more identifying with the ugly. No more morbid introspection that reveals who we were but not who we are.

Our identity has shifted. Flesh may be something we have and sin may be something we do, but neither is who we are. We can look away from the no-longer-I and turn towards God, who shows us our real and glorious identity. With delight and relief, we can shift our focus from the ugly to the excellent. With relief and delight we can focus on being new.

Rest

We can stop our efforts to get life and glory. There's no need to get what's already been given. We are free to rest, relax, and relish the life and glory that's already there.

And love

This is the best of all. Getting over our self-centeredness. Noticing God and noticing others. Noticing somebody besides me. Now, finally at peace with our identity, we can be receptive to God and receptive to others – and love them well.

NOTES

CHAPTER 23 – BEING WHO WE ARE

1. The Bible repeatedly calls God (both God the
    Father and Jesus, our rock. Some examples include:

    *Deuteronomy 32:3 For I proclaim the name of the LORD; Ascribe
    greatness to our God! 4 The Rock! His work is perfect, For all
    His ways are just; A God of faithfulness and without injustice,
    Righteous and upright is He.*

    *Deuteronomy 32:18 You neglected the Rock who begot you, And
    forgot the God who gave you birth.*

    *Psalm 18:2 The LORD is my rock and my fortress and my
    deliverer, My God, my rock, in whom I take refuge; My shield and
    the horn of my salvation, my stronghold.*

    *1 Corinthians 10:4 and all drank the same spiritual drink, for
    they were drinking from a spiritual rock which followed them; and
    the rock was Christ.*

2. *Cling* comes from the Hebrew work *dabak*, which relates to the
    modern Hebrew (Israeli) word *glue*. That fits. We're to stick to
    God as if we were glued to Him. References include:

    *Deuteronomy 10:20 You shall fear the LORD your God; you shall
    serve Him and cling to Him...*

    *Deuteronomy 13:4 You shall follow the LORD your God and fear
    Him; and you shall keep His commandments, listen to His voice,
    serve Him, and cling to Him.*

    *Joshua 23:8 But you are to cling to the LORD your God, as you
    have done to this day.*

God is our rock. We are to cling to Him.

•

Take my yoke upon you, and learn from me,
for I am gentle and humble in heart; and
you shall find rest for your souls.
Matthew 11:29

24
Being Me at the Airport

You need to know three things about me before this story will make sense: I have allergies, I loathe humiliation, and I was going to take a trip.

First the allergies. Every so often my allergies go crazy and I get a very sore throat and lose my voice. My voice doesn't just get quiet; it goes away. Completely. People laugh and tell me how great it must be for my husband, living with a wife who can't talk. Ha, ha. Ha, ha. Ha. I don't laugh with them, partly because I don't find it very funny and partly because it would hurt to laugh. I do at times manage a weak smile.

When the kids were little and my voice was gone I would be the only mom in the neighborhood standing at the front door banging a spoon on a pan to call my kids in for dinner. Yelling was not an option, and mouthing words out the front door does not get kids from the end of the block to the dining room table.

All this was frustrating. And also embarrassing. That's the second thing you need to know: I flinch when I even think about being humiliated publicly. Standing out like a sore thumb, being different (as in weird), calling negative attention to myself – I loathe them all. Which brings me to my trip.

I'd arranged to take a trip. My husband (the one supposedly thrilled that I couldn't talk) was in England on business and I (still in the States) intended to join him after his work was done. His side of the ocean was doing well, but my side of the ocean, specifically the allergy part, was acting up. I was a mess. I could talk a little, but had to cover my face with a mask, a big ugly conspicuous charcoal mask, whenever I left my air-filtered house. Home was no problem; home was my cocoon. But travel was something else altogether. Staring observers lurked in every airport, airplane, hotel, and tourist site. Travel scared me stiff.

You'd think, assuming a modicum of normalcy on my part, that I'd worry about the trip because I might get a lot sicker. That did cross my mind, but only as a minor issue. My real alarm centered on wearing that bizarre mask in public and having people stare at me. I knew it would happen. Every time I thought about it I started to sweat.

THE PARALLEL PLOT

In another part of my life, parallel to all this agitation, I was looking at Matthew 11 – the part where Jesus was saying He was

humble in heart. I began pondering the idea of humble and trying
to figure out how that worked. How exactly does one "do" humble?
How did Jesus "do" humble?

I started going over the Gospel stories and His humility was easy to
see. Jesus never tried to be more than He was and never tried to do
more than He was supposed to be doing: He showed His disciples
what it meant to serve as He washed their feet; He comfortably ate
dinner with people that the elite hypocrites avoided; rather than
using His power to call for angels to rescue Him, He submitted to
the cross. Humility upon humility.

But then there was the other part. Jesus didn't just avoid more; He
also avoided less. I started going through the Gospel stories again
and found incident after incident where Jesus could have settled for
being less than He was and He wouldn't do it, even when people
got really angry with Him. Pilate asked Him if He were the Son of
God and He said "Yes." People worshiped Him and He accepted
it – even though He knew that only God should be worshiped. He
stood openly on the mountain and gave Peter and John and James
an unveiled view of His glory. He even applied God's name (I AM)
to Himself. Is this humility upon humility? Yes it is.

Jesus' behavior unsettles our psyche because we think humility
requires walking slowly with eyes on the ground and head hanging.
Going around claiming He was God sounds not humble but
mockingly proud. Unless it's true. If it's true then Jesus isn't putting on
airs; He's simply agreeing with the reality of who He is. And no less.

Jesus never claimed privilege and He always asserted truth. Both
eating with sinners and claiming His glory show us His heart. He
never strove for more than He was, and never settled for less than
He was. He was who He was, and that's all. No more, and no less.
What a humble, true – and odd – way to live.

Living Oddly

No more, no less. I loved it. The whole concept was extraordinarily restful. And it seemed entirely unrelated to this trip looming before me. I was wrong.

I had a decision to make. Would I go or would I stay? Go out in public or hide? Deal with stares or keep myself out of sight and comfortable? I had to choose, and pretty quickly; we had two more days to either cancel or confirm my ticket.

I've learned that when I have trouble making a decision it usually comes down to one of two problems: either I don't have enough information (not the problem this time) or I'm unwilling to cooperate with one of the alternatives. God started asking me pertinent questions. *Are you willing to stay home?* Yes! *Are you willing to go?* That's when I started resisting. *Are you willing to go if I want you to go?* I struggled and hemmed and hawed and sweated, knowing all the time that I'd end up yielding – I hate defying God much more than I hate being stared at. People's approval is comforting, and His approval is necessary. *Are you willing to go if I want you to go? Yes, if You want me to, I'll go.* Once I yielded the choice was quite clear. Still distressing, but clear – I'd learned humiliation all too well. I was about to learn humility.

I started packing dark clothes so I would be less noticeable. The clothes matched my mood. Then it struck me – no more, no less. Just like Jesus. I didn't have to be more than a person wearing a bizarre mask, and I didn't have to be less than a woman made glorious by God. I took out a bright outfit for the plane ride. (I also chose a matching scarf to wrap around my mask. I decided my camouflage looked quite stylish.)

BEING ME AT THE AIRPORT

Burdened with three pieces of luggage (and some serious anxiety), I parked the car, wrapped my stylish scarf over my mask, and started my long walk to the gate. It was horrible. Every few yards, every few seconds or so, the strap on my heavy wardrobe bag would slip off my shoulder, my scarf would slip off my mask, people would stare at me like I was an carnival freak, and my hold on dignity would just slip away. And I'd have to stop to rearrange my luggage and my scarf and my grasp on who I was.

I kept re-teaching myself humility: *I don't have to be more than I am; I don't have to be less than I am.* And my awareness of inner dignity would return for a few more yards and a few more seconds. Then it would happen again: bag slipping, scarf slipping, dignity slipping; bag repositioned, scarf rearranged, identity reclaimed.

I didn't have any dollar bills to rent a cart and no one offered to help. The airport strangers just stared. And I kept walking my public gauntlet – alone except for God and Matthew 11. It seemed like miles to the gate.

Then a tall lanky man with an easy smile came up to me and asked if I wanted help with some of my luggage. "Oh yes, thanks a lot. I really would." I had to work to speak up since the mask muffled my already quiet voice. It didn't seem to bother him at all. He said he was meeting some people arriving later but had plenty of time to walk me to my gate. He put the heavy wardrobe bag on his left shoulder and I walked on his right. As we walked and chatted I mentioned how bizarre it was to be stared at and that I'd never been treated as an object before. It was a light conversation in spite of the subject, particularly since his easy way thoroughly relaxed me. He seemed to understand.

When we finally arrived at my gate I thanked him for his help and he turned away to go meet his friends. That's when I saw his left arm. It ended halfway down with a spray of fingers coming out of his elbow. He knew. Knew about being different, about being seen as a freak, about being treated like an object instead of a person. He'd experienced it himself.

I never noticed if people were staring (at him or at me) when we were walking together; I was too busy enjoying his company. But I bet they were staring, and I bet it was at both of us. He knew all too well about people's degrading stares – and about walking through those stares with dignity. With dignity. Not with hiding, not with humiliation, not with shame, but with humble dignity. He'd learned humility: he didn't have to be more than he was and he didn't have to be less than he was. Neither did Jesus. And neither do I.

No more ... no less. Oh Lord, You sent me such a humble teacher, so perfect for my need. Sometimes I wonder ... did You send me an angel?

Breinigsville, PA USA
15 June 2010
239920BV00001B/8/P